Echoes

— A Memoir —

Remembrance & Ruminations of a Life Well Lived

Alan Churchill

Copyright © 2010 by Alan C Churchill Publishing LLC
All rights reserved
Printed in the United States of America

Library of Congress Control Number 2010911228

ISBN number 978-0-615-39216-5

Dedication

This book is dedicated to the most important people in my life—my family. This includes the following:

Roscoe Sheller, my grandfather, who started writing even later in life than I have. His many books led the way and set the pace for the rest of the family.

Sam Churchill, my father, who put food on the table our entire life by writing. As a young boy, I didn't grasp the importance of what he was doing but now as an adult, well, it really is true that our parents get smarter as we grow older.

Dorothy Churchill, my mother, who constantly encouraged me to pick up the pen (laptop) and "just get started".

Sue Drummond, my sister, who beat me to the market with her own book thereby forcing me to get started. Sibling rivalry still exists 50 years after our youth.

Linda Churchill, my wife, who stayed with me all these years in spite of my weirdness. She also was very understanding when I would go into my "writing cave" for days at a time. Always supportive and always helpful; this book wouldn't be in your hand without Linda's help.

Flint Churchill (son) and Katie Knapp (daughter) who provided me with lots of material for this book and a lifetime of love.

I love you all.

CONTENTS

Preface 1

Acknowledgments 3

I Know I Can 5

The Ultimate "Growing Up" House 7

The Fort 10

The Challenge of the 7th Grade 15

The Challenge of the 8th Grade 17

Passing My Ham Radio Exam 20

The Science Fair 23

The Desk 24

Antennas 26

Summer Work 31

My First Car Phone 34

Grandview Avenue Grocery 36

The Party at Robin Paisley's House 38

San Francisco with Jerry Stein 40

Mexico and the Milk Truck 44

Breaking In to the State Police 47

New York World's Fair 51

Rick Lloyd 54

Freshman Class President 56

School Spirit and the Cannon 58

The Move to Seattle 61

Dirty, Hungry and Tired 64

Boy Meets Girl 66

The Fire 68

Sliding Doors and Flying Saucers 70

The Journeyman Test 74

Becoming a Land Baron 76

The Proposal 78

Campout on Saddle Mountain 81

Hawaii 84

The Walk to U of H 87

Back to School 89

Keith and Keith 91

The Rose Place House 93

The First Job 96

Burroughs 98

Flint's Arrival 102

The Bouncing Baby 105

Katie's Arrival 107

Katie, Jon and Scissors 110

Timberline	112
Mike Ayersman	115
What Price Success?	117
Dimensions	119
Moving	121
Writing Your Own Book	123
Permissions	125
Lessons Learned	126
About the Author	133

Preface

This book is all about "experiences". It is categorized as a memoir, which differs from an autobiography. A memoir can leave out sections of a person's life and allows more "creative writing" in the body of the work. This book was written over a period of approximately six months and it was a very enjoyable experience. My father, Sam Churchill, was a writer most of his adult life and he always said that to write, you just have to sit down and *write*. And he was right. But the wonder of it all was that the stories would come back to me as I just sat and thought about my life. I found that I could just let my mind "zone out" and pretty soon an experience would come back to me that would be worth writing about. Many times I would have to fill in the blanks by interviewing people I knew "way back when" and that brought forward even more memories.

The title came to me one night as I was reading a story about ham radio operators who were communicating by bouncing their signals off the moon and back to the earth. It struck me that pulling these experiences out of the distant past memory was like an echo. I would start to think about a time of my life and pretty soon, something would echo back to me. A little piece of memory would be jogged. Then I would fine-tune my thinking and the echo would become louder. Finally I would have a whole event on paper.

I believe anyone can write his or her own memoir and I encourage you to try. An experience forgotten is no better than an experience that never happened. Reliving these events was sometimes more fun than the original event.

This book covers only sections of my life and I cannot verify the accuracy of every statement. Most names are correct (these are real people) but dates may be a little vague. I hope you will enjoy reading this book as much as I enjoyed writing it.

Alan Churchill

Acknowledgments

When I started writing this book, I believed that the actual writing of the book would be the bulk of the effort. But, as any author finds out, there are more steps to getting a book published than just putting the words on paper.

I would like to thank Linda Churchill and Dorothy Churchill for their help with dates, people, places and, in general, the facts of the story.

For proofreading, I greatly appreciate the help of our "coffee group" which includes Don and Jerroll Shires, Bob and Karen Morris and Bob and Dona Worsley. Sue Drummond, my sister, also helped with proofreading.

Robert Knapp, Katie Knapp, Karen Morris, Jerroll Shires,
Dona Worsley, Bob Morris, Linda Chuchill, Bob Worsley, Don Shires

Roscoe Sheller, Alan Churchill

For all the technical details I would like to thank the entire staff at Gorham Printing. They published a book titled "A Guide to Book Printing and Self Publishing" and I referred to it constantly for several months.

I would like to thank my Dad for providing a role model that allowed me to believe I could do this.

And, finally, I would like to thank all the people that I mentioned in this book who made my life so interesting. You may not have realized that I was making mental notes when all these things happened but apparently I was. Now it is your time to worry about what I remembered. If you find yourself chomping at the bit to refute my memory and want to set the record straight, I recommend that you skip to the end of the book and read the chapter where I discuss the steps to publishing your own book. For those of you that don't want to write a whole book on my flawed memory, please feel free to email me at alan@alanchurchill.com with comments. I will get around to writing back to you when I have the garage cleaned up.

Dorothy Churchill, Linda Churchill and Susan Drummond, editors

I Know I Can

It wasn't really that far—maybe a little over three feet—but it sure seemed like it would be wise to get a long run at it.

Maybe it was the fact that the wading pool was made of cement. Maybe it was because Dad had drained all the water out of it to patch a leak. Maybe it was because I had never attempted to jump the pool before. Maybe it was because (only moments before), I had attempted to throw a one-quart glass milk bottle over it and the empty pool was now littered with broken glass.

No. Those weren't the reasons I was nervous. I knew I could jump it and land safely on the other side if I could just get up enough speed. I was a fast runner. The real reason I was nervous was that there wasn't anyone there to confirm my feat of superior running and jumping ability. Yes, I was sure I could jump the wading pool. All the experience of my five years of life was behind me. I could almost outrun Dad when I needed to.

I thought about whom I could get to watch my epic event (and prove that I really did jump all the way over the pool). My brother was only three so he would probably look away at the wrong time. My only other sibling was my sister and she was five years my senior. I thought she would probably be getting married soon and be moving away so I didn't ask her. No, in the end it was just *me* that would witness this event.

So here I was on a beautiful sunny summer day in Sunnyside, WA in 1950 standing 20' from my wading pool. I backed up to 30' then 40' to get a good run at it. No witnesses. Broken glass (lots of it). I crouched, studied the ground before me and *took off*. I felt like an Olympic runner. My feet barely touched the ground. It was really more like flying than running. As I came closer to the concrete pool with its shards of glass lying in wait I felt no fear—no doubt even. I knew I could *do it*.

I was wrong.

Years later in junior high, the scar on my leg was still very visible and that scar gave me a lot of boasting time with the girls when we were in PE. They would want to know *what happened* and I would brush it off as no big thing. Just a few stitches—maybe 10 or 20—I can't remember. I would throw in that I vaguely remember walking to the hospital on my own to get stitched up. That one scar brought me a *lot* of girl talk-time and it instilled in me the knowledge that regardless of how horrible the present circumstance is, there may be some good to come of it later in life.

The Ultimate "Growing Up" House

When I was six (well, almost), my Dad took a job at the *Yakima Herald-Republic* newspaper in Yakima. This meant we moved from the house on the hill in Sunnyside (with the now-removed wading pool) and made the leap to the big city. The house we moved to turned out to be where I would live for the next 13 years. My entire school life from the first to the twelfth grades would be spent in this house. I don't know if my parents ever considered it to be their ultimate house but for me, it was the Ultimate Growing Up House.

There were many features about the house that made it just perfect for a kid growing up.

1. It had a flat roof. When I was younger this wasn't such a big deal but when I started wanting to prove my manhood, jumping off a flat roof was just somehow "special". Also, flat roofs always leak. This meant we got to learn all sorts of new words from our parents (mostly Dad) when water would once again start dripping down the light fixture in our parents' bedroom. This also meant we got to spend a lot of time on the roof each summer playing with black roof patch tar. That stuff is great.

2. The house had a central core of closets with other rooms surrounding the core. This meant we could open all the doors and run at full speed in a circle inside the house. This activity was enhanced considerably when Dad would bring home a huge spool

of Teletype paper tape. A roll was about one inch in width and 1,000 feet long and came in several different colors. We would put a pencil or a kitchen knife through the center and run like mad around the "racetrack" until the paper tape was completely unwound. We could get about 20 complete circles out of one spool. This was great fun but Mom insisted we roll the paper tape back up before finding some other activity. That always took a long time.

3. The house had a basement with a *huge* furnace that looked like an upside down octopus. This taught us the feeling of stark terror when we would have to go downstairs alone at night. We had a wood-burning fireplace and for some reason, Dad stored the firewood downstairs behind the furnace. Since it was my job to haul wood I had to go down there a lot on winter nights. My sister, Susan, would wait until I was all the way downstairs then turn the lights off. That furnace was the scariest looking thing that a little kid could imagine.

4. The driveway, as well as our entire street, had a pretty good slope. This meant we could always get started on a new bike and could ride *fast* once we got our balance. It also allowed us to drag steel chains behind our bikes and they would throw sparks at night.

5. The back yard backed up to Pat Healey's house. Pat became my girlfriend in high school and that meant an easy commute for late night visits.

6. The house was small (about 1,500 square feet) and that meant we were together as a family. There simply wasn't enough room to get isolated so we learned to co-exist.

7. The living room had all hardwood floors. This meant we could roll up the carpets and have dances when we were in high school. People with wall-to-wall carpets just couldn't compete.

8. The electrical system was old so it always needed some improvement. Dad showed me how to install electrical plugs and switches. The electrical service was too small for the house so we learned how to use a penny as a substitute for fuses. Later in life when I became an electrician I would learn this wasn't such a great idea.

9. The house had a laundry chute, which went from the upstairs bathroom (there was only one bathroom for all five of us) down to the basement where the washer and dryer were. This laundry chute was to prove useful as a raceway for my many wires that needed to go from the basement to the upper floor. It is also where my brother Sam and I tested the theory that you can drop a cat down a laundry chute and it will land on it's feet in the basement (on a pile of laundry for safety). Sam and I also used it to drive our sister crazy when she was in the bathroom. We would stand directly beneath the laundry chute and, using two broom handles taped together we would push up on the lid to the chute. This would make her think we had climbed up the chute and were spying on her. Girls don't like that so we thought it was great.

10. And finally, the basement did not have a finished ceiling. This left the floor joists open for running wires, drilling holes, hanging things and in general, just making it better. When a basement ceiling gets covered up, a lot of fun is taken out of the room.

The Fort

The Hackenmillers were our next-door neighbors at the 24th Avenue house in Yakima. Mom and Dad Hackenmiller were "good" Catholics and by the time we were teenagers, they had one kid of just about every age. There was never a shortage of playmates thanks to Mr. and Mrs. Hackenmiller. The oldest child (Ronnie) was two years older than I so he was the boss on most things. One day when I was about ten, we decided to build a fort out behind our garage. Not just *any* fort, but a two-story fort complete with giant posts at each corner. We had a pretty good selection of building materials at our house but we lacked one of the corner posts. Fortunately, Ronnie came to the rescue. He had a 16 foot long 4x4 in his garage and offered to "loan" it to us. Since the other three corners were just 2x2 and 2x4s nailed together, Ronnie's 4x4 post was the only one that had real strength. It turned out this was a necessity.

So, with lots of neighborhood help, our fort was completed in just a few days. To give more headroom on the bottom floor, we dug out the dirt so it had at least five feet of head clearance. To get to the upper floor we built a 2x4 ladder. Standing on the second floor was just wonderful. We could see over the fence into the neighbor's yard (where attacking forces would have to come from) and we could even see down into several other back yards. It was the perfect defensive position—a high point for surveillance and plywood walls for protection.

The only real purpose of a fort is to defend against an attacking force so as soon as the fort was finished we addressed this need. We split up all the neighborhood kids into two armies. Ronnie was the captain of the attacking force and I was the captain of the fort. Each side had six to eight kids so it was just like a real army. Since Ronnie was the oldest kid, he picked mostly the older boys for his army. I got the smaller boys and even some girls *but*, I had the protection of the fort. In our army, we had enough people to dedicate someone to the manufacture of mud balls, someone to deliver and stack the mud balls and several of us to throw them at the opposing team. Henry Ford could have taken manufacturing lessons from us.

Well, the fort turned out to be the ultimate in defensive tactics. When Ronnie attacked, we could see him and his forces 50' away as they came around the corner of the neighbor's garage. We had all our mud balls lined up on a table on the second story so we had lots of ammo. When the other side hit us with a volley we just ducked down behind the plywood walls. When we decided to attack, all we had to do was stand up and throw mud balls one after another from our seemingly endless supply. In fact, since the mud ball manufacturing plant was the basement of the fort, our supply lines were short indeed. We even had a garden hose feeding the manufacturing facility so we had nearly an endless supply of mud. We could stay supplied with mud balls until the manufacturing group dug to China.

The opposing team, however, had serious tactical problems. They had to carry their supply of mud balls nearly 70' from their manufacturing facility behind the neighbor's garage to the battlefield. This meant that we could pelt them continuously as they attacked then continue to "finish them off" as they retreated to get more supplies. It was a completely one-sided battle. To add insult to injury, we found that our garden hose was long enough to pull up to the second floor and we could squirt the attacking forces with water. It was *great*. Ronnie fought a good battle but the fact was that we soon had his forces soaking wet and without supplies. We had won.

But victory wasn't to be long appreciated. After the waving of the white flag by Ronnie's forces, Ronnie came forward and wanted to switch sides. Switch sides? No way, Jose. He wanted us to give up our fort so we could be the attackers. This wouldn't work. Now Ronnie knew all our tricks. The mud ball manufacturing plant in the basement, the shelving on the second deck to hold an ample supply, the water hose secret weapon. No way. This was *my* fort. It was behind *my* garage. It was on *my* land. It was made (mostly) with *my* wood. Besides, all the people on our side were dry and happy. All the attackers were soaking wet, muddy and mad. Why would we ever want to switch sides?

But Ronnie was older and he had been saving his secret weapon for when he knew he might need it.

"I own the main support for your fort. I own the 16' 4x4. And, either we switch sides or I am taking my 4x4 back."

"Well it is a part of *my* fort. You *gave* it to us."

"No, I *loaned* it to you. I can take it back any time I want."

So now we had a standoff. Ronnie was bigger and his attacking force consisted mostly of his brothers. I, on the other hand, got most of the younger kids and some girls because we were better protected. I knew in a real fight, I couldn't have won. But it was *my* fort. I had designed it. I had swung a hammer and sawed boards for hours to build that fort. I quickly took stock of our remaining lumber supplies and realized that if Ronnie were to remove his support post, we would have nothing to replace it. But I also knew that if Ronnie did take the post, there would be no fort for anyone—him included. I bet that he was bluffing.

"So go ahead and take your ugly old post but then you will *never* have a fort to play in. You will *never* know what fun it is to have the strategic advantage. You will *never* get to know the fun of using the garden hose from five feet above your opponents." Ronnie looked at me and pointed out that I was refusing him these advantages anyway so why shouldn't he just take his post and go home?

It was a standoff. Ronnie finally gathered his troops around him, talked quietly for a minute or so and then walked off the battlefield headed towards his house. We had won. Total victory. Fireworks and ice cream were in order.

But wait. Only moments later Ronnie and his gang reappeared but this time they all had tools. Hammers, shovels, pry bars, even a saw! And, they were headed straight to the fort! My worst fears were realized. Ronnie started prying off the plywood walls, hammering out the nails that held his post in place and then he dug out the dirt around his post. With a huge crash, he pulled his 4x4 loose and the whole fort collapsed. In the time it took me to put my ice cream dish down and run to get Mom, the damage had been done. The fort—only one day old - was history. Ronnie and his gang were carrying the post across our yard headed to his house.

My mind snapped. He couldn't do this. It didn't make any sense. Even though Ronnie was two years older and a head taller I tackled him full force. He dropped the 4x4 and started swinging. I managed a few good punches to his face before he even knew what was happening. But, then his extra size kicked in and he was on top of me, pinning my arms to the ground with his knees. He was yelling that it was *his* 4x4 and the loaning period was *over* and he had every right to take it back.

By this time, all four parents were outside to see what the commotion was. Mr. Hackenmiller pulled Ronnie off me and my Dad stood me up. The parents said we would each get time to explain our side of the story. Mine was obvious. Ronnie had *wrecked* our fort—a construction project that the whole neighborhood benefited from. It wasn't fair that Ronnie could just decide when the loan period was over with no regard to the consequences. Ronnie countered with the point that I was unwilling to let him be the captain of the fort even though his 4x4 held the whole thing up. In short, his generosity was not compensated.

The two sets of parents looked at each other and announced that it was a hot day and we would all be better off at the swimming pool. Ronnie would keep his 4x4 and I would have to find a replacement on my own. We wiped the blood off our faces (mostly my blood) and headed to the pool at Franklin Jr. High. By late afternoon all was forgotten. We later used wood from the fort to build stairs to the flat roof of our garage. This introduced us to the death defying joy of jumping from a high location. We could even see farther than we ever could from the fort.

From this, I learned that gifts sometimes carry "conditions" and that friends can become enemies and then friends again.

The Challenge of the 7th Grade

I didn't want to be in class that day. I don't even remember a day that I *did* want to be in Lee Bofto's class. But Mr. Bofto was my homeroom teacher and seventh grade was looking like it would be tough. Almost from the first day, Mr. Bofto and I didn't hit it off. I loved to make jokes in class. I couldn't sit still. I never did homework. In short, I was a major disruption to the classroom. Early in the year he made me sit all the way in front of the class because he believed I would cause less trouble up there. I had been unfairly singled out by Mr. Bofto as a smart alec troublemaker.

He was the football coach and I turned out for track, not football. I liked humor. He was humorless. I liked girls. He hated girls. It was hopeless. Since he was my homeroom teacher, I had him for *two* hours every morning. Mr. Bofto didn't like kids who didn't turn out for football. Mr. Bofto didn't like kids who made jokes in class that got the whole class laughing. Mr. Bofto didn't like *me* and he controlled me (or attempted to) by putting my desk right next to his. I don't mean just in the first row of desks. I mean *right next* to his desk. It was humiliating. I had my back to the class so I couldn't see what was going on. I had Mr. Bofto's eyes on me all the time. It was horrible and I was having a tough time seeing how this could come out as an advantage later in life. But of course it did and it wasn't much later in life either. It happened in the 8th grade.

I had survived a whole year with Mr. Bofto as my homeroom teacher. I don't even remember what he taught. Probably civics or history or something you can get out of a book. The football coaches never did teach any of the interesting stuff like physics or chemistry or literature. No, their minds were always on the next game and they couldn't spend their valuable thinking time on class work. So it was that I finally graduated out of the seventh grade and into the eighth grade.

Thank *GOD* that was over.

The Challenge of the 8th Grade

But it wasn't over. Somehow, I ended up with Mr. Bofto for homeroom *again*. On the first day he sat me down to have a man-to-man talk with me so that maybe we could get along better. I wasn't buying it. I didn't think he was interested in giving me another chance. In fact, he used me as kind of a "demonstration aid" for what happens to you if you screw up and don't pay attention in class. If the class got out of hand all Mr. Bofto had to say was "Does someone else want to sit up front?" It was the same as saying, "Look at this jerk up here. You disrupt my class and this is what happens." The entire class (except me) took his ranting to heart. As a result, Mr. Bofto's class was usually pretty quiet.

But back to the "life lesson" that I learned from Mr. Bofto. It was about half way through 8th grade. I was about as demoralized as a kid could be. I wasn't the star of the track team like I thought I would be. The scar on my leg (from the wading pool) was beginning to fade and anyway all the girls had already seen it. Lynn Dye, the coolest kid in school had offered to show me a neat athletic trick where he could flip me up in the air and do a 360 so I would land on my feet again. The trick just didn't work out as planned. I landed flat on my back and got all the air knocked out of me. And, it was right in front of a whole string of the prettiest girls. The *one* girl I wanted to go out with the very most in the world—Diane Davies—was right there in front. She looked down at me like I was some weird non-athlete who couldn't even do a flip with help.

So, it was shaping up as another bad year but then something wonderful happened. Mr. Bofto lost control of his room. I had made some cute joke and got some kids laughing. Others played off of it and pretty soon the whole class was in an uproar. Mr. Bofto just came unglued. He said in a loud voice (shouting, I think) that we were all about to see what happens when someone deliberately disrupts his class. He walked to the closet and got out his "hack stick" which teachers really did use in those days. He used it as a pointer and slowly scanned the whole class. It was instantly quiet. We all knew where that stick stopped would be the poor schmuck who took a beating just outside his door. Slowly, slowly the stick pointed to one troublemaker after another and then Mr. Bofto took a step backwards and pointed it at *me*. "OK Churchill, let's go outside" he said in a low menacing voice. I was scared to death. Mr. Bofto was *mad*. And, he was *big*. He coached *football*. He was *strong*. And he pointed that hack stick at me. Straight at me. Everyone knew what was going to happen. I was going out into the hallway with Mr. Bofto where nobody could see and he would wail on me with all his might. I would scream and would have blisters for weeks to follow—and they would be in a place where I couldn't get any "girl sympathy". I slowly rose from my "up front" desk and walked toward the door. Mr. Bofto gave the instruction to the class that anyone who wanted to get up out of his or her seat to see what was going on would be the next one in the hallway. Nobody moved a muscle.

Out we went. Mr. Bofto guided me out into the empty hallway and around the corner to the staircase. It was then that I got my life lesson from Mr. Bofto. He offered me a deal. He would hit the stairs with his paddle. I would then let out a scream. He would hit the stairs again and I would scream again. He said that he would do this five times and if I would scream each time *and never tell anyone* what had gone on out there in the hallway that he would not give me any real hacks. Even before he finished wailing on the stair step I knew I had won. Oh, I was screaming all right and I have never told this story to anyone else but I knew that I somehow had gained the upper hand. I had conquered the threat of Mr.

Bofto. I had risen above it and realized that I was a force to be dealt with in Mr. Bofto's mind. He *needed* me to help regain control of his classroom. All his football expertise, all his bravado, all his humiliating moves suddenly seemed somehow lessened. I was the one in control.

He had struck a deal with the devil and the devil was *me*. And, I *liked* it.

Passing My Ham Radio Exam

Actually, the seventh and eighth grades weren't all bad. It was 1958 and I was in the seventh grade when I got my ham radio Novice license. My call was KN7JYR and I was never so proud of any accomplishment as I was of getting that first license. A fellow ham that had been approved to give tests administered the Novice license exam. The Novice license was only good for one year though and that meant you had to study and take a much harder test to move up to the General class of license. Also, the Novice license was only good for Morse code and you could use only 50 watts of transmitting power. With the General class license, you could talk on a microphone and use up to 1,500 watts of transmitting power. I wanted that General license.

Back in those days you had to go to an official FCC (Federal Communications Commission) office to take the General class test. My best friend, Jerry Stein and I rode over to Seattle on the train so I could take the General test. Jerry explored old Seattle while I went into the official FCC office. It was impressive. It was intimidating. It was everything I thought the Federal Communications Commission would be—big desks with important people behind them. There were conference rooms, pretty ladies and books everywhere but nowhere did I see any *radios*. I kind of thought they would have had a lot of radios at the FCC but they must have been in another building.

Anyway, I took the test and *passed*. I had to know the Morse code and be able to send and receive at 13 words per minute. That is about the speed of talking slowly. The person who gave the test simply got out a Time magazine and picked a story and started sending me code. I was so nervous that I missed about half the letters while he was sending but I had time to "fill in the blanks" after he finished sending. Well, that was *easy* because he was just sending me a story out of Time magazine. I could guess the letters I missed. I have always felt a little guilty about that but nobody from the government has asked for my license back and I have had it 50 years now so I guess I am safe.

The theory part of the test was 75 questions on general radio knowledge. Things like "what is the purpose of an oscillator" and "about how much power would a 1,000-watt AM station use from the power utility". All of the questions were multiple-choice and of course there were always one or two that you *knew* couldn't be the answer so passing that test was pretty easy too. The Advanced and Extra class licenses that I took later in life were much harder. There you had to really understand radio theory

A typical ham radio station in the early 1980s. Alan's was first licensed as KN7JYR, then K7JYR, then N7NOA and finally AA7CV. Alan is still active on the air today 50 years after passing the Novice test.

to get the right answers. I wasn't ready for those tests yet but I had my General Class license and I was ready to *talk* on the radio. My call sign changed from KN7JYR to K7JYR. The N (for Novice) had been officially eliminated. I was one happy kid.

The Science Fair

Late in the ninth grade our school had a science fair. I brought some of my ham radio station and a tube tester to the event and set up a booth showing off my equipment. Science fairs are really for geeky people and are mostly attended by everyone from the science club.

I was standing in my booth waiting for my fellow geeky friends to come along and who should appear but Sylvia Davidson. Sylvia was the most beautiful person in our class. She, of course, got straight A grades, dated the football captain, and in general seemed to be about six levels ahead of the rest of us in junior high. She was gorgeous. She even had breasts (which I was starting to notice). I thought she looked like a movie star. She dated only older guys (10th graders and the like).

Needless to say, I was stunned that she would come to the science fair let alone to my booth. But she did. And she showed interest. She wanted to know how my tube tester worked—or at least that is what I thought. So, after some time spent on filament voltages, plate currents and a thorough discussion of screen grids, she thanked me for a wonderful update on all things electronic and floated on to the next booth. I couldn't believe it. I had *talked* to Sylvia Davidson but more importantly; she had listened to what I said. I was in a dreamland the rest of the day. I can't remember who won the prize for the best booth or best whatever but I knew that my social status has bumped up a notch or two with my friends. After all, I had *talked* to Sylvia Davidson.

Life was getting more interesting.

The Desk

My Grandpa Sheller used to own a Ford car dealership in Sunnyside—just 35 miles from where we lived in Yakima. Consequently, we saw a lot of him and Grandma Sheller. Grandpa Sheller always showed an interest in my ham-radio activities. The wobbly desk of my ham station was built with the lumber left over from the (now dismantled) fort. It was nothing very fancy and pictures of my ham station never made it into the radio magazines.

All this changed on Christmas of 1963 when Grandpa Sheller presented me with a huge desk for my ham station. It consisted of two 4'x8' sheets of ¾" plywood joined together to form a desk size of 8' x 8'. He had cut out a huge semicircle on one side so that I could sit in my chair in the center and swivel around 180 degrees with easy access to all my equipment. It was *great*.

There was even room for rack mounted equipment on either side underneath the desktop. By this time I had some fairly big equipment - a 1,000-watt amplifier, and its associated power supply. Each of these two items was 20" high, 20" deep and 19" wide. The power supply weighed about 120 pounds and the amplifier weighed something less but it was wonderful to have a place for them all enclosed and safe. My mother had worried about me being electrocuted from the day that amplifier came in the back door. She had good reason to worry. The operating voltage was something like 2,500 volts, which is enough to get anyone's attention. It used as much power as our clothes dryer and we couldn't run both those devices at the same time. We were afraid that the pennies in our fuse box would just melt.

With the addition of some shelving across the back of the desk, I had all my QST and CQ radio magazines displayed handsomely along with all the other station accessories I had collected by that time. Any commercial radio station manager would have been impressed with my desk.

It may have been my imagination but I think my signal got out better once that desk was installed.

Antennas

By the time I was 14, my ham radio hobby was really progressing. I wanted to string up a dipole wire antenna over 24th Avenue. Our across-the-street neighbor was James Elam and he really liked electronics so he granted me permission to climb his tree and connect one end of the wire antenna to it. The maple tree was huge and stood at least 70' high. It made a perfect support for the far end of my antenna. Since 80 meters was my favorite ham band, the antenna had to be 132 feet long. Our lot was only about 80' deep which meant that going over the road to the Elam's big tree was the perfect solution. Fortunately there were no power lines going down our street—only telephone lines. This meant I could throw the end of the wire antenna over the telephone wires safely.

Getting the antenna wire across the street was something else again. 24th Avenue was the only road that connected Summitview Avenue with Lincoln Avenue for over a mile. This meant it was a busy street. The problem was, I had to throw the antenna wire over the telephone wires then somehow pull it up into the big maple tree before any cars came along. Since antennas work better the higher they are, I wanted to get as high up in that tree as I could. I climbed to the top branch, tied the rope off and threw the rest of the rope down to the ground. Now came the hard part. I had to connect the support rope to the antenna wire then pull the antenna up all while no cars came along.

Since 24th was so busy during the day I chose nighttime to do this work. At 11PM I made the connection of the rope and the wire and laid the wire down across the road. I was climbing the tree as fast as I could when I heard the dreaded sound. A car was coming. My wire antenna was lying across the street. Of course the car could just drive over the antenna wire but what if it got hooked to the underside of the car somehow? I climbed faster. At about the 25' mark, the car passed over my antenna wire without snagging it. Whew. I got to the place where I had tied off the rope and pulled like crazy to hoist the wire up into the air.

Once the antenna became airborne I knew I was safe. I climbed down the tree to inspect my work. There it was; a beautiful 80 meter antenna 50 feet over 24th Avenue. Of course I couldn't actually see it because it was pitch black dark. In the years that followed, I had many excellent contacts using that antenna. The antenna finally fell down in a windstorm several years later but by then I had my tower.

To a ham radio operator, a tower is a wonderful thing. It supports antennas that are rotatable which means that you can "point" it at the person or place you wish to contact. The beam antenna that sits atop a tower has gain in one direction only. This means it amplifies the strength of the signals in the direction the beam is pointing and minimizes the strength of all stations elsewhere. Unfortunately, towers and beams are expensive. By this time I had many ham buddies and one of them just happened to be putting up a taller tower and a new beam and he had his old ones for sale. I was able to trade him some equipment and a little precious cash for his old 30' tall tower and used beam. I was in heaven.

I started the installation process by convincing Mom and Dad that a tower and beam were basically the most wonderful things a ham could have (a necessity, actually). Once Dad got on board (Mom never did) we dug a hole for the concrete base. It was about two feet high, three feet deep and two feet wide. It turns out that a hole that big takes a *lot* of cement. I remember mixing bags of cement most of the day and filling the hole with concrete and rebar. The next day was set aside for erecting the tower. Of course, the base of a tower must be very level. If you get a tower started off on an angle at the base, you will have a big problem once you get 30' in the air. I didn't want my tower to look like the Leaning Tower of Pisa. With a lot of leveling of the soft concrete and later hammering with a maul we got the support base level.

Fortunately, we had positioned the tower right next to our house, which meant that I could stand on our roof for assembling the first two sections. The tower was in ten-foot sections. Of course the first section was easy—it was on the ground. The second section was almost as easy. I just stood on our flat roof to hold the tower section and Dad bolted it to the first section using a ladder. The third section however was something of a challenge since it was about seven feet above the roofline. We decided that we could bolt the tower to the side of the house. I still just love it that Dad would allow his kid to put big bolts right into his house. We could then lean a stepladder up against the tower from the roof. I know

This is a good example of the kind of antenna system that Alan really wanted. His beam antenna consisted of only one of the beams shown above. This "antenna farm" belongs to Stan Griffiths, W7NI.

this doesn't sound too safe but Dad was helping so obviously it passed his "collateral damage" test. By this time I was used to jumping off the flat roof, which was about 13' off the ground. I figured that (worst case) I would have to jump from about 17' if something went wrong. That seemed doable so I climbed the stepladder with the third tower section in hand and somehow got it secured to the second section. And there it was. A beautiful 30' tower ready for my new beam antenna.

We completed the tower with a set of guy wires at the 25' height. The thing stood straight and strong. I climbed to the top using two of Dad's old leather belts for a harness and took pictures of the view. It seemed I could see forever. In fact, I could see all the way to the end of our street! I just knew that stations from all over Europe would be easily accessed with a tower this high.

The next part of the tower project was to install the rotator which is the motor that turns the beam around. I had purchased an old prop pitch motor from military surplus. It was out of a B17 bomber and I figured that anything strong enough to turn the prop pitch on a B17 was strong enough to turn my little beam. I was right. If that motor had ever become "caught up" I think it would have twisted the whole tower around in a circle before it would stop. It weighed about 50 pounds so it was a *bugger* to get up to the top of the tower but using ropes and pulleys we finally got it positioned. Now the only thing left was to get the beam installed.

A beam antenna has a boom (a piece of pipe about 20' long) with multiple elements that are positioned diagonally on the boom. My beam had three elements. The whole thing had to be assembled on the ground and the elements checked for correct spacing. Then a vertical mast is connected to the center of the beam. The vertical mast must be lifted up and over the top of the tower and inserted down into the rotator, which is usually about three feet below the top of the tower. So, the problem is that you have to carry this whole assembled beam up the tower with you then lift it up over your head and insert the mast pole down into the center of the tower. Count the hands that are needed. You need two hands to hold on to the tower and two hands to lift the beam up over your head. Since I couldn't convince anyone else to climb the tower with me, I chose to simply wrap a big chunk of rope around my chest and through the tower to act as my "holding on" hands.

The only mistake I made during this process was to let my Mother know what I was doing. She stood in the back yard wringing her hands so tightly that she could have crushed golf balls.

Once the tower was finished and the beam installed I had many good ham radio contacts with the new antenna. I could point the beam at Europe and make contacts just about any time I wanted. It was great. That beam antenna turned out to be the best antenna I ever had.

Summer Work

Growing up in Yakima meant there was always summer work. From sixth grade almost through high school, I was kept busy mowing lawns and doing yard work. I started with just a few "senior citizens" who no longer wanted to mow their own grass and ended up with pretty much a full time job for the summer months. Each year I would add a few more homes to my route. At first it wasn't too much work but as the years progressed and my clientele grew older, I was asked to do jobs that were much more strenuous.

One of those more strenuous jobs was with Mrs. Harriet Parker and later her daughter who came to live with her. Mrs. Parker had a *huge* lawn and wanted her lawn mowed with a hand mower. She was dead set against the "new fangled" rotary mowers that ran on gas. Also, she didn't believe in using a grass catcher as it somehow caused the mower to not mow evenly. So, the drill was to mow the lawn, then rake it, then mow again. All by hand. All in 110 degree heat. I pegged Mrs. Parker's age at around 100 but young people always guess high so in retrospect, I would guess she was probably around 70 when I was 12. She paid me $1.25 an hour to mow her massive lawn. The second mowing was always "gratis" for some reason. Furthermore, her house was a good three miles from where I lived so I was usually already hot and tired by the time I walked there. It took about four hours to do the mow, rake, mow project. She also had me trim the edges with a hand trimmer. Nothing electric would do.

In spite of this, I liked Mrs. Parker. After my morning workout, she would always bring out a big pitcher of lemonade and cookies and we would sit in the shade and talk. She had many stories to tell of her husband and their life in San Francisco when they were young. In fact, her daughter came to live with her when I was in the 11th grade and she was from San Francisco too. Between the two of them, they made me want to go to that big city.

When I turned 16 I worked at a radio repair shop. This was definitely better than mowing lawns. I loved radios and found a place called Glencourt Electronics that needed a "gofer". This was back in the days when people would still get their radios and televisions fixed when they broke. I was put in charge of the initial dismantling and dust cleanout of the sets in preparation for the actual fixing stage, which was done by someone else. I learned a lot about TV and radio repair from the owner, Wally, and would later use that knowledge to start my own repair service.

There were two things that usually would cause a set to stop working. 1) bad tubes and 2) bad capacitors. Both of these were easy to diagnose. At this time in electronics, tubes pretty much had one purpose. So, if the TV picture continuously rolled up or down, I went looking for the vertical amplifier tube. If the screen was all black, I would replace the rectifier. If there was a lot of "noise" on the picture, I would look at the big filter capacitors. Before long, I found that I could have about half the sets fixed before the technician would get to them. It was great fun to see what I could do.

My pay at Glencourt Electronics was not in cash. Our agreement was that I would get $2 per hour (way over lawn mowing rates) but the payment would come from the value of items I selected from the owner's junk pile. The owner and I would negotiate the value of each piece I wanted at the end of the week. Sometimes I would get a non-working TV chassis with lots of usable parts. Sometimes it would be a working radio. One week a customer brought in a *huge* speaker and amplifier that he didn't want. It was about 30" in diameter and was in a floor standing cabinet.

The amplifier put out about 100 watts of audio power which meant it was *loud*. As soon as I saw it, I knew I had to have it. It took about two weeks of work at the store to come up with the needed bank account to buy that speaker and another three weeks of work to have enough to buy the associated amplifier. I borrowed the family station wagon and brought my two beauties home and took them directly to the basement for testing.

I carefully plugged in the speaker and a turntable to the amplifier and moved the switch to ON. Nothing. I checked the tubes, checked the connections, and looked under the chassis. Everything looked good. I turned up the volume control to 50 then 75 then all the way. The output tubes were now glowing blue but still no sound from the giant speaker. I then decided maybe there wasn't a good connection from the turntable to the amplifier and I pulled the RCA jack out of the back of the amp.

And that is when it happened. An RCA plug has a central "hot" pin that extends out beyond the grounding shield that surrounds it. This means when you pull out an RCA plug from its jack, you lose the ground first. This leaves the central pin (the hot side) still connected. A huge BRAPPP sound came from the speaker and I watched as the considerable audio power from the amplifier tore the speaker cone to shreds. Then, with the speaker wires melted together, the expensive final amplifier tubes both blew up. In one second I had destroyed what took me five weeks of work at the TV shop. There was no saving it. The speaker was totally destroyed and the cost of new amplifier tubes exceeded the value of the amp. I just sat there with my mouth open looking at my lost amp and speaker and calculating what the hourly cost of one second of sound had cost me. And, it wasn't even a good sound.

From this I learned to always keep the volume control low when working on electronics.

My First Car Phone

Around the 10th grade I finally got some money together by doing yard work on the weekends and running my paper route during the week. This "hoard of cash" enabled me to purchase a ham radio station for my car. Now, this was *cool*. It operated on the 2-meter band. The rig (ham talk for transmitter/receiver) had a small control head that allowed me to operate the whole thing from the front seat. The transmitter/receiver was large and took up most of the trunk of my parents' car. Why they allowed me to cut holes in the roof for the antenna and in the firewall for cables is still beyond me. Probably I said something about emergency communications and how we would be the only family in Yakima to survive when the local Army firing center blew up. I don't know. The problem was that the mic (microphone) just looked too much like a police radio to be cool. I wanted something like a telephone handset to talk on.

So, one day while Mom and Dad were at work and I was skipping school, I took apart our home telephone. I knew that the handset had both a mic and speaker and I reasoned that I could connect the handset to my new mobile ham rig. This meant I could drive down the road and look like I was talking on the telephone! How cool was *that*? With just a little work with the drill, I was even able to install a push-to-talk switch so I could operate the whole thing from the handset. I made it a habit of driving around with the windows down so people could see me talking on the phone while driving along. In 1962 that was a *big* deal. I loved it. The fact that the station was installed in a 1958 Ford station wagon that belched blue smoke took something away from the coolness but I still liked it.

The only downfall was that I had to come up with an excuse why our home telephone no longer had a handset. I was able to steal one from my junk box to put the home phone back in service but Mom and Dad didn't ever think it was acceptable and asked me to check with them before utilizing items around the home for my ham station.

Grandview Avenue Grocery

When I finally got my driver's license, I got a job at Grandview Avenue Grocery. My job was to deliver groceries to the clientele that Lloyd and Anne Harris had built up over the years. The deliveries were made to two groups of people—rich people and old people. The rich people bought things that I had never seen before. Lloyd and Anne had tweaked their inventory as the years went by to cater to the "weird" things that rich people ate. Seasonings from France and Italy were common. I saw my first jar of Pickled Pig's Feet at Grandview Avenue Grocery. The breads had to be super fresh. Anne would throw out anything that was over one day old. All the bread at our house was over one day old because we got everything from the day old bakery. I couldn't imagine why people needed bread that fresh. Besides, unless they ate a whole loaf of bread the first day, they always ended up with day-old bread!

Part of being successful at grocery deliveries is to do it quickly so I found that I could use some of the built-in features of the delivery truck to my advantage. One of those features was that the engine was so old that there was almost no compression left in it. This meant I could turn off the engine about 30 feet away from a house, jump out the door while the truck coasted and be opening the back door at about the time that the van rolled to a stop. This worked OK on a level street only. Once Lloyd asked me how I did deliveries so quickly and I mentioned my methods. His face whitened somewhat and the very next week he bought a new delivery van. The new van had good compression so I couldn't use my "jump and run" tactics. This actually hurt my speedy delivery times but Lloyd never complained.

The other method I used to speed up deliveries was to use my horn when backing out into traffic. I found that if I just did a "toot, toot, toot" as I backed out into a street, people would stop for me rather than me waiting for them. Yes, I put a lot of trust in my fellow man but it always worked out.

Except for once.

I was backing down a long driveway doing my toot, toot, toot thing when all of a sudden there was a loud crash. The owner of the house I had just delivered groceries to was a passenger in a car that had parked right across their driveway. I backed straight into the side of the car right at the passenger's door. Fortunately she had not started to get out yet so nobody was hurt but the door didn't look like it would open. The owner of the car jumped out and started exclaiming about how her car was *totally demolished*. She pointed out not only the caved in door but also other bumps and scrapes on *all sides* of the car. Some of these dents and scratches had rust on them so I knew that I couldn't have done all that damage. However, Lloyd soon arrived on the scene and assured the lady that he would fix her car and that there wouldn't even be a delivery charge for the customer's groceries that day. I started to explain to Lloyd that I couldn't possibly have done all the damage the lady was claiming but he apparently had good insurance and wanted to keep things cool. Fortunately this took place before we got the new van.

From that point on, my "trust of my fellow man" was modified to "trust but verify (that nobody is back there).

The Party at Robin Paisley's House

One of the girls that I looked at a lot (but never spoke to) in high school was Robin Paisley. She lived on the hill in a house that seemed so big we referred to it as "the mansion". Robin was from another space and time. She observed all the rest of us at Eisenhower High School rather than being a part of us. We never knew her well since she spent much of her time at private schools and on extended vacations with her parents. However, she was very pretty and of course she had an older boyfriend. Well, the boyfriend somehow knew where the spare key to "the mansion" was and since Robin and her parents were gone so much, the house was empty on many occasions.

If you put together an empty house, a key to that house and a teenage boy, there has to be trouble in the next sentence. And there was. The boyfriend decided it would be OK to "borrow" a little of the ample liquor supply that Robin's parents had. But he needed help. He called a friend and that friend called another friend and pretty soon there were 15 or so kids at Robin's house drinking their liquor. Well, things got totally out of hand and the guys decided to go swimming in the pool. And they forgot their clothes. And they neglected to notice it was well past 10PM. And then the police decided to get in on the fun.

So, by about 1AM, all the most popular boys of our high school were sitting at the police station thinking maybe drinking all of Robin's parent's liquor wasn't such a good idea. The thing was, they had *so much* liquor that it was hard to tell just how much they had consumed. Well, it must have been enough because when the Paisley's got back home, all Hell broke loose.

The judge met with Mr. Paisley and the two of them decided that a fit punishment would be for all 15 boys to work a month in Mr. Paisley's business. That may not sound so bad but Mr. Paisley owned the local meat packing plant. They made hot dogs there and you *know* what goes into hot dogs. The guys were (of course) assigned the absolute worst jobs and in a meat packing plant there are some really *bad* jobs. I am sure Mike from Dirty Jobs has turned these jobs down. So, by the end of the month all 15 boys were *convinced* that they would never drink again (at least at Robin Paisley's house). They would all go to college and become college professors or some other profession that would *never* be involved with meat packing. All in all, it was an excellent application of "time fitting the crime" and it also made for endless stories for years afterward.

I heard that Robin broke up with her boyfriend.

San Francisco with Jerry Stein

It was the summer between my junior and senior years at Eisenhower High School. Jerry Stein and I had been planning a trip to San Francisco for some time. Jerry had an old 1937 Plymouth into which he had recently installed a brand new battery. So, we reasoned, it was now in top shape (even with 110,000 miles). The car was a perfect "road car" because the front windshield cranked out and the wing windows cranked all the way around to catch the air for air conditioning. The hood covers folded up under themselves to allow better cooling of the engine. It had a huge back seat for food supplies and even a trunk for extra cans of oil and water which were a necessity.

We picked San Francisco because we could get there with only two days of driving and that was where Sandi Dolph and Susan Kellinger had moved to earlier in the year. Both Jerry and I had been in love with Sandi before she moved and we each considered her our girlfriend at one time or another. Neither of us had dated Susan but she was *hot* and we both liked the thought of seeing her again.

So, with the hood folded in and the front windshield cranked fully out we set off for San Fran in June of 1963. From Yakima, we took Hwy 97 down to the Columbia River then down highway 197 to Bend, OR. We stopped to see Peterson Rock Gardens and had lunch then headed on to Grants Pass where we camped in amongst the giant Redwood trees. It was great fun. People honked and waved at us as we motored along at our maximum speed of 50MPH. Some of them were waving with only one of their fingers.

I don't remember much about our campout that night except that we probably ate pretty well. Our mothers worried about their babies out there all alone so it is reasonable to think that they would have made something really good for us. Also, since the trip to SF was just two travel days, we figured we would be eating at Sandi or Susan's house the following night so there was no reason to hold back and save food. It was a good eating night.

The following day was *hot* and as we passed over the summit between Oregon and California we started to smell something burning. We were pretty sure it wasn't all *that* important because we had used only half our oil supply and had filled up the five gallon water container just that morning. Plus, we had a full set of tools in the trunk (a hammer and a screwdriver). However, the burning smell continued and we decided that we had better check it out. By this time we were in the middle of nowhere. It was hot and there were very few cars passing us, which meant there were very few other cars because *everyone* passed us. We pulled over and did a visual check. Fortunately, we found that it was a minor thing. The rope we used to hold the engine hood together had fallen down onto the engine and was smoking up a storm. Since we had the windshield cranked out, we got all the "engine smells" first hand.

It was a good thing we stopped when we did because fire was probably only minutes away. Also, since we had driven about 50 miles, it was time for another gallon of water in the radiator. We figured the leaks in the radiator were good because only the hot water leaked out leaving the cold water in the radiator. I don't think either of us did well in physics in our junior year but ignorance is bliss.

About 4PM, we rolled into San Francisco. We had agreed to meet Susan at her home and all our expectations about Susan and food were exceeded. Her parents invited us in and fed us well. Since we had virtually no money, we had made no plans for where to stay. Fortunately, Susan's parents casually said during dinner that we were welcome to stay at their

Jerry Stein in 1963 with the Plymouth we went to SF in.

place if we would like. Much to their surprise, we said *yes*. We ended up staying three days and three nights and it was *great*.

After dinner that first night, Sandi came over and we spent the evening exploring San Francisco. Jerry naturally matched up with Sandi and I got Susan. She was so beautiful—tan and thin and rich (which some say are the three staples of life). I was overwhelmed and I am sure she was counting the minutes until we headed back home. We spent most of the three days we were there in her swimming pool. We had heard that all California girls loved to swim naked during the day while their parents were at work but that didn't seem to be the case with Sandi and Susan. Jerry and I were severely disappointed.

After four days with the girls it was time to explore the big city on our own. We had heard of "the crookedest street in the world" and went in search of it. We had been having some trouble with the brakes in Jerry's

37 Plymouth (there weren't any) so we were trying to stick to fairly flat roads. Unfortunately, in San Francisco, there are very few flat roads. By this time we were using the hand brake as much as the foot brakes. Well, we found the crookedest street in the world but it also turned out to be one of the *steepest* streets in the world. As we edged over the top of the street it looked to us like it was a near vertical drop. It took all the foot brakes the old Plymouth had left plus all the emergency brakes plus a new method of braking that we hadn't thought of before to get to the bottom of the hill. The third method involved rubbing the tires along the curb. That method was somewhat scary because, for some unknown reason, people did park on this street. This meant we had to dodge around them, which meant we gained a lot of speed while we had only the other two braking methods available. Everything worked out well though and we made it to the bottom of the hill.

Our week in San Francisco finally had to come to an end. Even with the food and lodging help of Susan's parents and the entertainment of a swimming pool, we had burned through nearly all of the $100 we had brought with us. It was time to head home. We discussed the issue of not having brakes but I pointed out that we were headed North for the remainder of the trip and that meant we would be going up hill most of the way. Jerry agreed and we made it safely back to Yakima with the Plymouth no worse for wear. Jerry was able to replace the brakes himself once he got home and the 37 Plymouth gave Jerry many years of service after that.

One last note on the Plymouth. Rick Lloyd bought the car from Jerry several years later and he still has it stored in a barn in Minnesota. Rick and his wife Kate now live in Bend. Who knows; Jerry and I may fly back to Rick's place in MN and drive the old Plymouth home again. I think we might check the brakes first though. I wonder if the battery is still good.

Mexico and the Milk Truck

It was our junior year in high school and four of us (Robin Rieder, Dave Helland, Rick Lloyd and I) decided it would be a great idea to go to Mexico in celebration of our high school graduation. Of course we couldn't afford to stay in motels and none of us had a vehicle big enough to take four guys and all their stuff so we had to find a suitable vehicle. We pooled our money and came up with $200. We determined that this should be enough to buy a good large vehicle. We found an old 1951 International milk truck in "ready to fix" condition. Fortunately, Dave Helland had a friend who owned the Chevron station on ninth and Yakima Avenue. He let us park the milk truck right next to the station and use his mechanic tools for the few "fix up" things that needed to be done.

We decided to break up the repair into areas of responsibility. I was responsible for the electrical system. Dave was responsible for the engine. Rob was the tires and transmission guy and Rick was the trip planner. Dave actually was pretty good mechanically so he soon got the engine working. I replaced much of the wiring as it had been eaten by the previous occupants—mice. Rob found new(er) tires and mounted them and Rick spent time at the library looking up where girls stayed when they went to Mexico. We wanted to be sure and be near those places.

After about four months of work the truck was ready. We painted *Mexico or Bust* on the side and spent our last pennies to fill the tank with gas. It was time for the maiden run of the newly improved Milk Truck.

So off we went with Dave driving and the rest of us standing in the back (there were no seats other than the driver's seat). We made it all the way up Yakima Avenue and turned down 24th to show it to my parents. They were strangely skeptical that our milk truck would make it to Mexico the following summer. We knew it would last "forever".

Forever turned out to be less than a mile more. It was my turn to drive so I adjusted the driver's seat (which was a wooden apple box) and away we went. At the top of our street I turned left onto Summitview Avenue. As I turned, something caught my eye in the left rear view mirror. For some odd reason I could see the rear tire plainly—all of it. And, it was becoming more visible as we continued around the corner. By the time I got straightened out I could see that we had real problems. The whole wheel and axle was coming out of the side of the milk truck. Somehow we had forgotten to assign "rear end" responsibilities to anyone and sure enough, that oversight meant that we had found the weak link in our otherwise complete repair process. Well, I was screaming pretty loudly about the wheel coming out of the rear end but nobody else could understand because they were all in the box and the box had no windows. I rolled over to the side of the street and stopped. We all got out to see that, sure enough, the tire, wheel and about half of the axle extended out from the side of the truck into one of the two lanes of Summitview Avenue. Since we didn't have things as basic as a jack in the milk truck, I ran back to my house and got one from my parent's car. Within a few minutes we had the truck jacked up enough to push the axle back into the rear end but of course that didn't mean we had solved the problem. We decided to coast down Summitview until we could get to a place where we would have enough room to work on the rear end. Susan Gould's house was on 20th just off Summitview and we decided that since she was gorgeous, she wouldn't mind if we parked in front of her house for a while. It was slow going but it was downhill so (with a sharp eye on the rear view mirror) we coasted the four blocks down to Susan's house. Fortunately, the problem was on the left side of the truck so we could just edge over to the side of the road. Susan lived on a dead end road and that meant that we wouldn't have many cars driving over us as we lay in the street.

Since Dave was the best with mechanical things, we left the analysis phase to him. I don't know if I ever knew what the problem was but Dave figured it out and with a loan from our parents we got the truck back in operation within a few days. This additional "work time" meant we had time to visit with Susan while Dave worked on the rear end. We didn't mind the hours of effort because we got to talk to Susan.

Several days later the truck was back in pristine condition and our "test drive" continued. We went to each of our houses to show it off to our parents and friends.

And, that is as close to Mexico as we ever got.

The problem really was Rick Lloyd. In doing his research, he determined that we would use about $150 in gas just getting to Mexico and back and that at the maximum Milk Truck speed of 50MPH, it would take about two weeks each way. That would burn up our entire budget for money and time and we wouldn't even get to see any of those girls in Mexico. So, the whole idea was dropped except that now we had a Milk Truck to sell. Dave's friend let him keep the milk truck at his gas station while we attempted to sell it - which turned out to be over two years!

I don't know if the new owners ever went to Mexico in the milk truck but it was ready.

Breaking In to the State Police

It was now October of 1963. Our senior year of high school was well under way and Jerry Stein and I needed a break. We decided to take an exploratory Jeep ride up into the mountains. Both Jerry and I were fairly accomplished at mountaineering in that we had both camped out a lot. So, forgetting everything we ever learned about preparation for a Jeep trip into the mountains, we decided to head up into the Cascades for the afternoon. There was no need to tell our parents where we were going because we would be back long before dinnertime. I brought a candy bar and Jerry brought some stale donuts from his kitchen and we were on our way.

The first suggestion that we might have prepared better came when we got stuck in a snow bank and realized we didn't have a shovel. We also didn't have any more food since the donuts and candy were gone before we hit the city limits of Yakima. Of course this was long before cell phones existed so we had no way of contacting anyone. Nobody knew where we were and we were now miles from the nearest living human and it was starting to get dark.

It was time for a conference to do a little strategic planning. Since we were too far from the main road to walk out and since we had no way of dislodging the Jeep, we decided to hike up to the top of the nearest peak and have a look around. We still had enough light to see a little ways. Thirty minutes later we were standing on the highest point for miles around and right there on the peak with us was a thing of beauty—a cement block building with humming noises inside and a bunch of antennas on the roof. We had come across a radio repeater installation of some type. After a thorough inspection we determined that there was no way in. The steel door was locked solid, there were no windows and the building was sturdily built. But, the building offered us the heat we would need to survive the night. We needed some way to get inside.

And then we spied it—the building's Achilles Heel. There was an air intake grate near the bottom on one wall and it was just about big enough for us to crawl through if we could somehow dislodge the grate. Off we went back to the Jeep to get any pry bar or other tool we could find. Jerry happened to have a nice hammer in the jockey box so we brought that back along with some sturdy branches to use as pry-bars. It took about 40 minutes but we finally got the steel grate torn off the building. We crawled into the 10' by 10' building to find racks of radio equipment. One of the panels had a microphone hanging on a clip and being a ham radio operator I knew that we had just struck gold. We had *communication* with the outside world. We still didn't know whose equipment this was or who would answer. I took a deep breath, picked up the microphone and said "Hello? Can anyone hear me?" After a short pause, an official sounding voice said, "Who is this and what are you doing on this frequency?" I explained that we got stuck in the snow and we were afraid of freezing to death in the cold night air and so we broke into this building and could he call our parents so they wouldn't worry and did he know if there was any food stored in the building because we were getting pretty hungry. After a long pause, the voice at the other end said, "This is the Washington State Police statewide repeater network. You are to touch *nothing* and say *nothing more* on the radio and you are to *not leave* the building and there is *no food* and (at last some good news) that someone would come to get us."

Well, he didn't sound any too friendly but we really liked the idea that they were going to send someone to rescue us. We decided to just sit down and wait. It had taken us about two hours to get to the building from Yakima so we were prepared for a long wait. It was only 20 minutes later when we heard what sounded like a helicopter in the distance. By then it was about 10PM and pitch black so we decided to stay in the warm building (like we were told). Then (and it was just like in the movies) the night lit up with the brightest helicopter spotlight I have ever seen and the loudest voice I have ever heard said *"come out of the building slowly with your hands on your head."* Holy cow. Did they mean us? This guy didn't sound the least bit friendly. We slowly opened the door, put our hands on our heads and walked into the blinding light. Somehow there were four four-wheel-drive pickups facing us with their high beams shining right at us. There were *lots* of guys in uniforms running toward us. Snow was blowing around like a gale from the helicopter blades. I wanted to scream out "You'll never take us alive, Copper" but Jerry wisely said we should just be quiet and let them take us to jail forever.

It turned out that the state police were very concerned about the security of their radio system and two of them spent quite a bit of time checking dials and meters while we waited (freezing) outside with two other state policemen standing next to us. They let us put our hands down so at least we could put our hands in our pockets. Two other people were securing a temporary grate across the hole in the wall (where did they get *that* so quickly?) and all in all, there were about eight police people out there. I started to wonder if our families were going to get billed for this.

In the end, it all worked out OK. We got a ride to the state police office in Yakima in one of the pickups and our parents came to get us. It was about midnight when we got home and I don't think we ever got dinner that night.

We went back the next day with Bill and Reed Johnson in their Jeep along with lots of shovels, towropes, axes, camping equipment and food. We got Jerry's Jeep out of the snow bank in short order. Bill and Reed wanted to see the radio repeater building where we had spent a part of the previous evening but Jerry and I thought the police might have cameras and dogs and armed Gestapo around the building and we wanted nothing to do with it. We headed home none the worse for wear.

Looking back on this event, I am *sure* that the state police officers had decided to have some fun with us and used the terrorist language on us. At least someone had a good time that night.

New York World's Fair

Jerry and I had so much fun going to San Francisco in the summer of 63 that we decided to make a trip to NYC (since the Mexico trip was cancelled). We scheduled it for as soon as we graduated from Eisenhower high school, which was 1964. By now my parents had purchased a new car so their 1962 VW bug was available to us. We had considered taking Jerry's 1937 Plymouth but we wisely calculated that she just wouldn't make it through another long trip. We removed the back seat of the VW and installed a shelf to hold our supplies of food and camping equipment.

Our first stop was somewhere in Montana where we found an old dance hall. It was boarded up but with a little prying with our tire iron we found ourselves standing on the stage of the old abandoned building. It was complete with a long bar (no liquor) and about a thousand mice. We set up our sleeping bags on the stage and spent the whole night dreaming of dance hall girls and listening to the mice running around us. There was no running water so we broke camp early and found a public campground where we got a much-needed shower and had breakfast.

By the third day we had consumed nearly all the food in our cooler. The ice had melted a day earlier. The only thing left was a cup of cottage cheese that had now grown some colorful patches. We normally didn't eat any food that had green patches but we figured if we split the cottage cheese neither of us would be too sick and much to our surprise there were no bad side effects.

On the fifth day we rolled into New York City and we really felt like two country boys in the big city. We passed nearly-new cars on the freeway that had been stripped of everything—even the wheels. We decided that we would definitely *not* leave our car at the side of the road if we had trouble.

We stayed with two sets of friends of my parents while we were there. Looking back on it, they must have been very wealthy because their homes were large and elegant. The first place we stayed had a separate guest house where we slept. It was nicer than either Jerry or I had at home. They invited us to dine (not just eat) with them and they had also invited several of their friends. The dinner was formal and everyone was dressed up. The nicest clothes Jerry and I had were jeans but at least our hosts had allowed us to use their washing machine so we were somewhat presentable. The dinner guests made polite conversation with their new friends from "out west". I distinctly remember one elderly lady asking how the Indian problem was being addressed. I was confused so asked her which problem she referred to. Her response shocked me. She said, "You know, the attacks and such." She really thought that civilization ended somewhere around the western edge of New York state and beyond that there were still Indian Wars going on.

We stayed with those folks for three days. We went to the New York World's Fair during the day and saw many new inventions and displays. The GM Futurama show, which showed what life would be like in the future, awed us. It was the fair's most popular exhibit. We also visited the IBM exhibit showing the latest model 350 series computer—a wonder. We saw things like an electric toothbrush, the world's largest cheese (Wisconsin) and something called "audio-animatronics" presented by Disney. After the fair was over, the "It's a Small World" and "Carousel of Progress" Disney exhibits were transferred to Disneyland where they are still in use today. The Omnimover ride became the PeopleMover at Disneyland.

After visiting the fair for four days (not enough time) we drove north to Pleasantville to stay with Carolyn Rogers who was one of the editors of

Readers Digest. She was Dad's editor for several articles he had published in that magazine. She was very gracious and fed us well. She later came to Yakima for a visit. It was her first time to the West and she had an observation about housing construction. Her comment was "There is so much wasted space here. Why do they put so much empty land between each house?" I guess she was used to living in high-rise apartments and couldn't understand why people would build a house for just one family on ¼ acre.

Our visit to New York opened our eyes to a world much larger than Yakima, WA. It created the desire in both of us to see more of the world and that was to happen (in spades).

Rick Lloyd

All the way through high school, a whole bunch of us just kind of stuck together. There were the smart ones—Kim Vandiver, Pat Healy, Dave Harnden, Cindy Rider, Susan Gould, Sylvia Davidson and many others. Then there were the rest of us, which included Jerry Stein, Bill and Reed Johnson, Robin Rieder and Dave Helland. We all thought that college would somehow accept us regardless of our grades but that didn't seem to be the case. Having fun was just a little higher on the importance scale

Jerry Stein and Rick Lloyd get together to swap fond memories at one of our high school reunions.

than studying hard. So, when it came college time, well, the colleges didn't call like we thought they would.

Rick Lloyd was an active member of our continuous party at junior college. I got to know Rick while at Eisenhower since we lived kind of close to each other. Rick and I determined that junior college was incorrectly named. We thought a better name would be "location for parties after high school is over". And that is what we did. Rick was the ultimate "party animal". He would always show up ready for fun but Rick has some sort of odd "cleanliness thing". That is, regardless of where the party was, he would end up taking a shower and then rejoining the party clothed only in a towel. This was great sport for the girls to see who could grab a hold of Rick's towel first and cause the "unveiling".

I suspect some of the parents of the houses we partied in must have wondered who was taking showers in their house while they were away.

Freshman Class President

The junior college I went to was Yakima Valley Junior College. I selected it based on the fact that *no* other college would accept me based on my GPA. YVJC accepted me because; well, because they *had* to. It was a state law or something. The tuition was cheap ($65/quarter) and the education was actually pretty good (I was told).

The first thing I did at YVJC was run for Freshman Class President. I had been involved in school politics all during my high school years and enjoyed it a lot. Being in school politics meant you got a lot of time out of class and that appealed to me. YVJC had a student union building (which was really the cafeteria) but they said it "belonged" to the students. It was named the Tepee Union Building (or TUB for short). Yakima had many Indian names so none of us thought Tepee Union Building was at all strange. So, when it came time for a slogan for running for class president, I came up with

DO IT IN THE TUB
VOTE FOR AL CHURCHILL

Some of the faculty and even some of the students misunderstood this slogan. I was called in to meet with some of the faculty members to discuss my slogan which was now plastered all over campus. They pointed out that some people might be offended by the slogan. I was dumbfounded. The TUB is where the voting took place so if you were going to vote for *anybody* you would have to do it in the TUB. I had a really hard time being "confused" and they finally said that I should change the signs to read, "Vote for Al Churchill in the TUB. " I didn't like that slogan because it lacked a certain "punch".

Well, anyway, the meeting broke up with no definite instructions given to me but I knew they were "thinking about it". I had spent $15 getting 500 of those posters made up and I wasn't about to just throw them away. In fact, given the fact that the faculty thought that the slogan was so *bad*, that meant that it had to be really *good*. I immediately went back to the print shop and had another 500 made. That night a bunch of us got together and in just two hours we *plastered* the whole campus. It looked like those signs you see for prize fights where they just cover whole walls of buildings. It was great.

I won the election.

And then the fun started.

School Spirit and the Cannon

As a class president, I had the ability to spend some money on activities to "build school spirit". Wow, what an invitation to disaster that was. Our own particular form of building school spirit took the form of a cannon. We thought it would be really cool to fire off a cannon every time we made a touchdown at football games. We went searching the local pawnshops and found a great cannon that was in our price range (dirt-cheap). It was about two feet long and was bolted down to two railroad ties. It weighed about 150 pounds so it took two people to move it around. There was a ½" hole in the top at the back for loading gunpowder. We would wad up rags and ram them down the barrel of the cannon, fill the ½" hole with gunpowder and light the fuse. Actually, fuses were kind of expensive so we found that we could just pour the gunpowder in the hole then continue a little trail of it up the barrel of the cannon. We would light the powder and *run like hell*. The thing was incredibly loud and would blow the wad of rags the full length of a football field. Since our football team made very few touchdowns we didn't get much of a chance to use it but it sure scared the opponents when we did fire that thing off.

It was about the second football game when the fire marshal showed up to ask us some questions about the cannon. He was particularly interested in our gunpowder source and our method of lighting the thing off. I guess he didn't like our answers because right then and there he declared the cannon too dangerous to use in a public place and instructed us to stop using it. This seemed unbelievably unfair to the students (it was their money we spent) and to the football team (who all thought the cannon was *great*). But, authority is authority so we agreed to load it up into Stan Johnson's 1950 panel van (a retired delivery van from a local cleaner) and not use it at any more football games. This kind of took the fun out of our "school spirit" so several of us decided to leave and see what else was going on in Yakima that night.

And then Stan got a good idea. Stan was older (about three years of junior college under his belt) and he always had good ideas. He said "you know what? The fire marshal is gone. Maybe we should fire this thing off one more time just as a farewell salute". Wow. That made sense. We were now several hundred feet out of the parking lot but still close to the football field. The football players would *love* to hear that thing go off one more time and since we were now mobile we would have a quick get away. It was perfect. Rick Lloyd then got the great idea that we should leave the cannon in the van and just open the rear doors. Once the cannon fired we could close the rear doors and nobody would know who did it. We pulled off the road into the faculty parking lot and backed the van up so that the rear pointed at the playing field. We debated how much gunpowder would be enough and decided that a little extra was needed so that the sound would travel the extra distance.

All was now in readiness. The rags were punched down extra hard. The gunpowder ran all the way up to the front of the barrel to give us extra time to run. We braced the cannon against the back seat. The only decision we had to make was who would light the fuse. This setup was more complicated than usual in that the person lighting the fuse would have to be inside the van to light it then jump over the seat and out the door before the thing went off. This required quick action since the time between lighting the fuse and the time the cannon went off was only about two seconds. Not a lot of time to do the gymnastics. Rick Lloyd was elected because he was thin and quick on his feet.

Well, Rick didn't quite make it all the way out of the front door by the time the cannon went off. I think he suffered permanent hearing loss. The van, however, suffered more dramatic damage. The sides of the van actually ballooned out somewhat and the cannon blast took out one of the glass windows in the back of the van. Stan's van was still drivable although the doors never did close correctly after that and none of the lights in the dash worked. On the bright side, the sound was *unbelievable*. The van acted as a sound reflector and concentrator (just like my beam antenna) so that everyone at the football game heard the explosion. It was just the most awesome cannon firing anyone anywhere had ever heard. Unfortunately the police (a lot of them) also heard it and before we could even get out of the faculty parking lot they had us surrounded. We all went downtown to the police station and our parents had to come and pick us up. We never saw the cannon again and Stan took to riding a bike to class.

Based on this experience (and many others), Stan ended up being my Best Man when Linda and I got married.

The Move to Seattle

Based on my interest in things not related to attending class, I decided that I just wasn't "YVJC material" so I set my sights on Seattle. Seattle was a *big* town with over 500,000 people. Compare that to Yakima with something like 40,000 and almost everything about Seattle seemed magical to me. So magical in fact that I decided there was simply no reason to finish out the quarter at YVJC. I just left. I felt I saved a lot of time by skipping the withdrawal process. I used this extra time to have some "last parties" with my YVJC friends and before I knew it, I was on my way to Seattle in my 1962 VW Bug. This was the same car that took Jerry Stein and me to NYC only two years earlier.

    I arrived in Seattle with no job and no prospects for a job and no skills and no money. However, I did have my sister Susan (whom I now liked a lot) living in Seattle with her new husband, Ron. In fact, they were just back from their honeymoon. I rang their bell and they must have been surprised to see me because they both said, "What are *you* doing here?" I told them that I had decided to move to Seattle (just like they did) and "could I crash at their place for a few days (or weeks) until I found work." They looked at each other and agreed that a night or two could work. So, I was set.

    The first week of looking for work was kind of disappointing. Sue made really good breakfasts and at that time she wasn't working so we had lots of time to get "caught up". That first week just flew by but I hadn't really started talking to anyone about a job. At the start of the second week, Ron offered to drop me downtown so I could start interviewing. I thought that was really nice of him. On the way downtown he suggested that I start at the labor union for electricians. With my background in radio and my natural interest in all things electronic, that would be *perfect*. The closer we got to the labor union the more I wanted to be an electrician. I didn't know anyone there. I didn't have a resume. I didn't know how unions worked. I just walked in the door and the first thing I heard from the business manager was…

"I am sorry. We only open up applications one week per year." Geeze, what kind of a deal is that, I wondered? My next question was, "When is it open again?" The answer still mystifies me. He responded that *this* was the week that applications were being taken—and they would close tomorrow! "Well, *let's get going then*" I said. So, he gave me the application and I went into the union hall to fill it out. It took hours to finish the application but I handed it in and asked what the next step was. The business manager responded, "Someone would call me." Now, at least, I had a reason to stay at my sister's house for a few more days (weeks?). I then realized that I was in downtown Seattle and I was miles from my sister's house on Magnolia Bluff. I thought about walking but decided a call to Sue would be best. She was thrilled to hear I had actually talked to someone about going to work and came to pick me up.

I was so excited about possibly becoming an electrician that I went to the library and read everything I could find about the trade. I was *pumped*. And then the call came from the union hall that my application had been reviewed and they would like to meet with me. Boy, I couldn't get there fast enough. The hiring process consisted of a 60-day trial period where anyone I worked for could fire me for any reason at any time. I later learned that as an electrician (or any other trade for that matter) your entire working life is a "trial period". It was very normal for an employer to lay off workers when there wasn't enough work. Anyway, I did get put into the four-year apprenticeship program and headed out to work just a few days later. Ron, my brother-in-law was more excited about my employment than I was. He even offered to take me around to apartment buildings and check them out. He was a great guy.

Dirty, Hungry and Tired

The apartment. MY apartment. My *first* apartment. It was only a one bedroom and was on the ground floor so it was noisy but I was living on my own with a job and freedom. The apartment was right on Denny Way in Seattle just up from downtown so I was "close to the action". The only catch was that my job was about 45 miles away. It took over an hour to get there in the morning and about 1.5 hours to get back home. Downtown Seattle traffic is some of the worst anywhere and it was just as horrible then as it is now. I would get up at 5AM so I could get to the job site by 7AM. We worked until 5PM every day which put me back home around 6:30 or 7PM.

It was *hard* work. I mostly dug ditches that first year but some of the time the journeymen would let me help them "pull wire" which was a lot more interesting but just as hard. So by the time I got home and took a shower and had something to eat, it was usually around 8PM. That meant that my social life was pretty much non-existent. My friendships, quite naturally, began to form around my fellow first year apprentices. We had school two nights a week from 7PM to 10PM so if traffic was heavy, I would have to go directly to class from the jobsite. That meant I would be dirty, hungry and tired. We got one 20-minute break from class at 8:45PM and we all headed to the tavern right next door for a beer(s) during that time. This would have been OK but most of us were doing the same menial jobs—digging ditches, pulling wire or just running errands for the journeymen. The work in the first year of apprenticeship is just plain hard so we were mostly dog-tired. Add to that a couple of beers and no food and the second half of class was just a *killer*.

Fortunately the teachers that the union hired were very good and kept the class lively so falling asleep was usually not the problem. Learning anything was the problem. By the time we had been attending class for 6 months, the "break time" got somewhat stretched out. Twenty minutes turned into 30 then 40. Of course, the amount of beer you can drink in 30 or 40 minutes is a lot more than you can drink in 20 so the second part of our training was getting somewhat out of hand. Our teacher was a journeyman electrician and had gone through the same course we were in. He understood. He also had to lay down the law. No more drinking contests at breaks! No more 40-minute breaks! And then he threw in the final killer. He pointed out that if he were to go to the tavern and speak with the bartender about checking ID, the whole beer drinking process would come to an abrupt stop. He was right. None of us were 21 and we all knew that the bartender looked the other way (the place was a dive) and if he turned us away, he could go all night with no customers.

We all decided that one beer would be our limit and 20 minutes would be our break time limit. A workable peace continued for the remainder of our apprenticeship years.

We all learned more after the new rules went into effect.

Boy Meets Girl

By the time I had been in Seattle for a year, I had moved three times. I was alone in my first apartment and that was really cool but it was expensive. I started looking around for a roommate and happened on an old high school friend, Bob Cardiff. We both had the same money problems so we moved into a place not far from where my first apartment was. Bob had a serious girlfriend so I almost never saw him. After about six months, he decided it was crazy to pay for one place and live elsewhere so he abandoned me for a better option. So, there I was paying full boat again. I found another friend, Roy Robinson, to be my next roommate and moved again. So, one year, three addresses.

The place with Roy really was better anyway. It was on the third floor of an apartment building right on the edge of Interstate 5 in downtown Seattle. We had a great view from our walkway. On some weekends, Roy and I would move our chairs out onto the walkway, lean back, drink beer and watch the world go by.

One day a new girl moved in. We sat on our walkway drinking beer and watched her move box after box of belongings into her second floor apartment. When it looked like she was done moving boxes (and we had run out of beer) I decided to go down and introduce myself. She didn't seem to be impressed with me but over the next few months we starting to see more of each other. I didn't know it then but this girl (Linda) would end up being "the one". She had decided to take a year off from Western

Washington State College and come to Seattle to make some money. She was smart, a real looker and I liked her right away.

Our first date was in the summer of 1967. I put the top down on my red 1962 Chevy Impala and we were off to the movies. We never got there. I was preparing to turn left in a large intersection when I glanced down at Linda's legs. Hmmm. Very nice. The next thing I knew there was a very loud crash. My car was spinning in circles in the center of the intersection and Linda was clear over next to the door. Another crash and she was sitting practically in my lap. I had started turning left in the middle of the intersection and had not seen the VW bug coming toward me. He hit me right on the rear axle going about 45MPH. The police later told me I spun around three times before crashing into one of the cars that was waiting at the red light. Even though neither of us was wearing seat belts (it was 1967 and they didn't exist), we had no injuries. The VW driver, however, was badly hurt. The entire front of his VW was compressed right up to the windshield. We later learned that he had just been released from the hospital after a serious car wreck. The crash with us put him in the hospital again for three months. The second car I crashed into wasn't damaged too badly and they ended up taking us home after the ambulance, tow trucks and police left. So, as first dates go, ours was quite memorable. I don't think I even got a good night kiss that night but there would be more opportunities.

Although my car really didn't look that bad from the outside, the VW had broken my rear axle and bent the frame of the car. The insurance company declared it a total loss. After a few tears, I went shopping and ended up with a cute little Volvo which I later traded for a 1956 Thunderbird, which was a *great* car for picking up girls. However, as summer grew into fall then winter, I found that there was only one girl I wanted with me and that was Linda. We had our first kiss on Christmas night 1967 and things just got "all crazy" after that.

The Fire

After about six months in the apartment with Roy, he got married so I was (once again) stuck with the whole rent payment. By this time, I had made friends with Doug Wilson who was a fellow apprentice. Doug lived with a bunch of guys in the U district (University of Washington). Relocating with Doug meant I would cut my rent payments to almost nothing. This seemed like a good opportunity so I moved into the last available bedroom in Doug's house. The reason it was empty was that it faced the street and our "across the street neighbor" was the fire department. This meant I was the first one to know whenever there was a fire or other emergency in our area. And this turned out to be a good thing.

The feeding arrangement at Doug's house was structured. We rotated cooking responsibilities among the five of us—each person had a full week of cooking the evening dinner. Breakfast and lunch we were on our own. One of the guys (Graham) just LOVED peanut butter and jelly sandwiches so for an entire week we had peanut butter and jelly sandwiches for dinner. One of the other guys was really quite a good cook so during his week we had casseroles and other "fancy" food. On my week we would BBQ. I loved to BBQ and in the summer, it was always burgers and chicken and beer. On the weekends we would start the "beer part" around noon and would eat at around 4PM. This meant that by the time we got started with firing up the BBQ briquettes we were all pretty well lit ourselves. Saturday was the day that Doug mowed the grass (since he was the owner it was his responsibility). The rest of us were sitting on the lawn having our fifth or sixth beer of the afternoon when I got the great idea that we should play a joke on Doug. The joke was that we would follow Doug while he mowed away from us and we would pour a trail of gasoline behind him right at the edge of the grass (next to the house). Then, when he turned around to mow back toward us, we would light the gas at our end and he would see a small trail of fire coming at him. We figured it would look something like a fuse used for dynamite.

We were wrong.

Maybe when I poured the gasoline "trail" I used a little too much gas. When I lit the gas there was a huge *whoosh* and instantly the whole side of his house was hidden in a blaze about eight feet high and about 30 feet long. Yes, Doug was surprised.

We now come to the part about "it was a good thing the fire department was across the street" because they were in our yard in about 30 seconds with fire hoses blasting. The loss was limited to a tree (which was growing too close to Doug's house anyway) and most of the paint on that side of the house. Once the fire was out we got a stern lecture from the fire captain on the dangers of mixing beer and gasoline. That seemed to take most of an hour. By the time the excitement was over we discovered that we had forgotten the BBQ and our beautiful burgers were now just black charcoal. So, since it was my week to cook, I decided to treat everyone at McDonalds.

That was maybe the best dinner we had that month.

Sliding Doors and Flying Saucers

I was well into my third year of apprenticeship when I was given an opportunity that every apprentice electrician dreams about—my own truck and jobs of my own. Granted, these were "dingbat jobs" which means little residential jobs where you really don't have to know much to succeed. Also, if you screw up a dingbat job, usually nobody dies, unlike large commercial jobs.

So, one fine day I was out on a residential job that had to set a record for "the simplest electrical job ever". The lady of the house wanted an outlet put in the wall in her dining room. This was a fine old turn-of-the-century Seattle home and was filled with rich cabinetry and expensive finishing details; a nice place. It turned out that the electrical panel was in the basement almost directly below where she wanted the outlet so the whole job consisted of cutting in an outlet box and connecting it to the panel with about four feet of wire. A 15-minute job.

There are a lot of little tricks that you learn from the journeyman electricians. One of those tricks is how to know where to drill a hole from a basement up into a wall cavity. It is pretty easy. You straighten out a wire coat hanger, put it in your drill motor and drill the coat hanger straight down right next to the wall where you want the hole to go. The coat hanger will act like a tiny drill bit and will create it's own hole. Once the coat hanger has gone through all the flooring you just go downstairs and look for the coat hanger extending out of the floor above. Then, you just move over a couple of inches and you can drill straight up right into the wall cavity. I had done this quite a few times and it worked every time.

So, the lady showed me where she wanted the outlet to be placed. I did my coat hanger trick and went downstairs. Sure enough, there it was sticking out of the ceiling just like I wanted. I moved my big ¾ inch bit over two inches and drilled straight up. Most floors are about 1.5" thick so it takes only about five seconds to drill a hole up into the wall cavity. But the drill motor just kept drilling and drilling with no end in sight. I figured that I must have hit the bottom of a stud so I moved off to the left about two inches and tried again. This time the drill worked for about 20 seconds but it did go through. Then, as I pulled the drill bit out of the hole, I heard what sounded like breaking glass. Odd, very odd. Why would there be glass in the middle of a wall? Well, back upstairs I cut in my hole for the outlet box, pulled the wire in and had it up and going in about ten minutes. A new record for a completed job. I went to find the lady of the house and showed her that the outlet actually did work and asked her to sign the work order as complete. She seemed satisfied and signed.

As we were leaving the dining room, she reached over to pull the sliding pocket doors closed. One of them closed easily. I noticed it was a beautiful mahogany door with glass panes in it. However, the other side just wouldn't move. She tugged on the little finger latch again but it was stuck. I had a sinking feeling in my stomach because I could see that my new outlet was about two feet in from the door opening. It turned out I had drilled a ¾" hole right up through her fancy pocket door with glass panes to install the outlet. These were *expensive* doors and I was not eager to see what I had done. I had no option but to remove the outlet I had just installed and try the door again. Sure enough, the door pulled out of its pocket just fine but right there in the middle was a monster hole and a broken pane of glass. The door was ruined. I called the boss and asked him what I should do (it was hard to hear him over the wailing of the lady) and he said he would send the estimator out. She asked me to leave. The boss asked me to leave. I wanted to leave. I never did find out what we paid for a replacement door (set of doors) but it had to be a pretty penny.

Another funny little incident happened during my third year of apprenticeship. I was out on my own again. It was a Wednesday and this was my first job of the day. If you ever want to hire an electrician, be sure to ask if the person that is coming attended apprenticeship class the previous night. Our training nights were Tuesday and Thursday. Since we always "stopped for a few" after training, Wednesday and Friday mornings were oftentimes filled with hung over workers. This was a Wednesday and I had really stayed out late with the boys the previous night. In fact, I don't think I was sober yet when I arrived at the lady's house. I was replacing her electrical panel, which is normally a pretty simple job. Step one was to disconnect the power to the house by pulling the meter off the wall. Step two for me was to go into the basement where I was to install the new panel. It was pitch black. In fact, by this time, my head was spinning around and my stomach was getting more upset every minute. I told the lady I was going to the truck to get a flashlight. Once I got to the truck I jumped in and headed straight for a diner to get some food in me. I found a Woolworth store with a lunch bar and sat down.

I needed food fast. I knew I couldn't go much longer before some of last night's beer was going to make a grand entrance. The waitress brought me water (much needed) and took my order for pancakes, eggs and toast. But, it was taking too long. Much too long. I figured I had about ten seconds left before I was going to empty my stomach right there on the eating counter so I did the only thing a thinking person would do. The guy just two stools down from me had a full plate of toast in front of him. I made a decision. I lunged for the guy's toast right in front of his face. The saucer went flying as I stuffed both slices in my mouth as fast as I could. Ahhh. Disaster averted. My seatmate's eyes were as big as the toast saucer, which had crashed on the floor and broken into a million pieces. I apologized profusely and explained that he really did want me to have his toast. The alternative was just too gross to contemplate. He agreed and I bought his breakfast.

Surprisingly my breakfast arrived soon after that. Then I ordered a second breakfast and finished that one too. My head had stopped spinning. My stomach felt much better. When I got back to the lady's house she asked why it took almost an hour to find my flashlight. I explained that flying saucers were involved.

She left me alone the rest of the day.

The Journeyman Test

The test. Well, no, really it was *the* test. It was the test we had to pass to become journeymen electricians. After four long years of going to school two nights a week and doing most everything a workman could do, we had to pass the state exam to become journeymen electricians. And, the test was a killer. Virtually nobody passed the test the first time and usually it took three to four times. If you failed the test you couldn't take it again for three months. That meant you couldn't collect full journeyman's pay for another three months (or six months or *nine* months or however long it took to pass). I heard of one guy who took the test *seven* times. That is almost two years! The normal pay scale for an apprentice was 50% of journeyman's pay for the first year then 10% more at the end of each succeeding year. That meant that fourth year apprentices usually made 80% of what a journeyman makes. A 20% pay raise was a *big* deal to me so I really wanted to pass that test.

At the end of our fourth year of class, our teacher brought a sample of a training guide to class. He showed us how it could be used as a prep guide for the test. The cost, though, was an astounding $450. That was almost a month's pay and nobody could afford it. I thought about extending my 80% pay rate by another three months or longer and decided the $450 seemed to be affordable. I took all the money out of my savings and bought the course. I then took off work the week before the test to study. When the results came in, I *passed!* And, I was one of a very few in my apprenticeship class that passed it the first time. That first paycheck as a journeyman electrician receiving full scale was a highlight in my life and it burned into my brain the fact that preparation paves the road to success.

To make my investment in the course even better, I sold the training guide to another apprentice who had failed the test. I got $300, which means my net investment had a payback period of about three weeks.

Becoming a Land Baron

It was about this time that the real estate market starting booming in the Seattle area. It seemed that *everyone* could become a real estate tycoon. In reading the Seattle Post Intelligencer, I came across an ad for five-acre lots on Whidbey Island for only $52.50 down and $52.50 per month. This was too good to be true so I decided that I needed to make a trip to Whidbey Island the very next weekend. The trip was fun—about two hours by car then another hour on a ferry and there I was in the heart of my very own island (or at least a part of it). The ad was factual. The price was $5,250 with $52.50 down and $52.50 per month. And, that price bought five acres of land and it was even kind of close to Puget Sound. It was too good to pass up so I plunked down my $52.50 and was on my way to being a land baron.

I had my tent with me so I decided to camp out on my property that very first night. It was heavily covered with brush, which made getting around difficult. Fortunately the surveyor lines were still fresh so at least I had a path around the perimeter of my land. Moving inland required some cutting with my hatchet. I finally found a good spot and set up the tent. Of course I had no water or food but the town of Coupeville was only a short drive away and had everything I needed. It was paradise. Here I was camping on my own land. There wasn't *any* noise (unlike at Doug's house with a fire siren every few minutes). There were a few other things that there weren't any of—water, restroom facilities, neighbors, etc. I loved it.

The master plan for the development included drilling a well for water and construction of some facilities. The well did get drilled but the developer never did find potable water so no cabins or other permanent homes could ever be built. It turned out that the property was to remain "uninhabitable" due to the lack of drinking water and therefore the value never did increase. About 15 years later I decided to sell the property. I listed it for $12,500. No takers. Not even any phone calls. I dropped the price to $10,000. Nothing. $8,000. Nothing. I finally reduced the price to $5250 and didn't get one bite. I then decided to price it at $12,500 again but put in the ad that I would carry the contract - $125 down and $125 per month. It sold in a week.

From this I learned a disturbing fact—some people pay attention to the monthly cost, not the total investment. I would use this knowledge many times in the years to come.

The Proposal

Linda and I had now been dating for about a year and I knew that my feelings for her were directing me toward wedded bliss. But, how to propose? I didn't want to do the "down on my knee" thing. I didn't want to ask her father for permission. I just didn't know what to do or how to do it.

It was September and Linda had decided to go back to college. She actually moved back to Bellingham, which was 100 miles from Seattle where I lived. I couldn't believe it. How could she leave me like this??? So, the weekly trips to Bellingham started. Sometimes Linda would come to see me. Most of the time I would go to Bellingham. I don't think we were ever apart for more than five days at a time but to me it seemed like forever.

Then it happened. It was February and Linda came down on the Greyhound for a weekend visit. I really hadn't planned anything. Any time with her was paradise and it really didn't matter much what activities were scheduled. So, when she got into the car I suggested we go to Northgate shopping mall and just wander around. The first place we came to was Friedlander's Jewelry and we looked at rings from the outside of the store. Then, just out of curiosity, I asked if she would like to go inside for a closer look. I really hadn't thought this out. I had no plan. In we went and Pete, the *nicest* salesman came over. In only moments he had us standing in front of the diamond ring case. Linda didn't see anything that really "rang her bell" so we ended up spending the whole day Saturday touring through diamond stores in downtown Seattle. Towards the end of the day, we found *the one*. She loved it. All at once I realized that this was shaping up to be an important day in my life. And then out of nowhere, I heard the salesman saying, "and how will we be paying for this, sir?" Uh, uh, *what*? Uh, check I guess.

So I wrote out a check for all the money I had in the world, which was way more than was in the checking account. I made a mental note to move my savings to the checking account the first thing Monday.

And so we walked (floated) to the car in the parking lot. We got in and looked at the ring on her finger and I realized that I had never asked Linda if she would marry me. What if she thought this was really just a very nice "friendship" ring? What if she just got carried away and didn't know how to say "no?" What if she had some guy at college in Bellingham that I didn't know about? Oh man, I had a big question to ask and it looked like now was the right time.

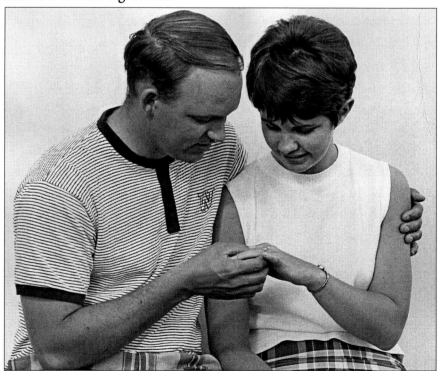

Alan and Linda inspect the engagement ring in 1968.

So I found myself saying, "By the way, would you like to get married—to me?" Fortunately she said yes and I let out a giant sigh of relief.

If I thought the proposal night was stressful, I had no idea what it would be like to make our announcement to her parents. We waited the whole week and didn't say anything. Then the following weekend, I drove to Bellingham and picked her up and headed to her family home in Edison, WA about 30 miles away. It had been a tough week and I was really sleepy so Linda drove to her parent's house. I woke up when we pulled into the driveway and instantly every potential catastrophe jumped into my mind. What if they said no? What if they were offended that I didn't ask permission? What if they had someone else in mind and wanted Linda to reconsider? There were very few good options that popped into my mind. On top of that, every family member and distant relative of the family seemed to be there. We walked into a house full of people and it seemed like everyone looked at us with some expectation. Linda saved the day by making the announcement in a graceful and romantic way. All of a sudden it was all hugs, hand shaking and toasts to the newly engaged couple. I was relieved and excited. Now we had only my Mom and Dad to see.

The following weekend we drove to Yakima and redid the whole "look what Linda has" thing. Fortunately just my Mom and Dad were home so it was a much simpler and less stressful event. All the families were genuinely excited for us. We set a date of November 23, 1968, which seemed like about four lifetimes away to me but at last I had the girl of my dreams and she had said yes.

The future was indeed bright.

Campout on Saddle Mountain

The whole "growing up" time at our household had included camping. Mom and Dad loved to camp and every summer (and some winters) we would be out in the wild. By the time I was 16, I think we had seen every campground west of the Mississippi. I loved camping. The whole family loved camping. Who wouldn't love camping?

So, when I suggested to Linda that we go camping as a fun thing to do together, I was shocked to hear her say, "Well, I *guess* that would be OK." Kind of like, "eeeuuuuu, but I like you, Alan, so I will go if you want to." I was perplexed that she would have this attitude about camping. I mean, what's not to like? You have the wonderful smell of the forest, the excitement of finding your own wood to build a fire, stories around the fire, and best of all, smores. Everything about camping is just wonderful.

So one day in late March, I decided that it would be a good time to return to Saddle Mountain where I had spent many campouts with my parents. The drive from Seattle was pleasant (although cold) and I used the whole trip to sell Linda on the joys of camping. Amazingly, she had done almost no camping during her childhood. I was going to be the one that introduced her to this wonderful way of life.

We got to the base of Saddle Mountain at around five PM. It was still light but it had gotten colder. As we drove up to the campsite (four miles) it seemed to get even colder. There was no snow on the ground (well, very little) so I knew we would be fine. We arrived at the campsite to find a rope across the entrance and a sign that said "campground opens in April". Well, obviously March was darn close to April so I figured the forest service people wouldn't mind someone jumping the gun by a few days. We unpacked our tent, sleeping bags, camp stove and other necessities and headed for one of the camp spots. Hmmm. They all seemed to be somewhat wet. And the picnic tables were covered with branches and slime. And there was no wood for a fire close by. Apparently, the forest service had a lot of work in front of them to open the camping area. But, I was a Boy Scout and gathering a little wood for a fire couldn't be all that hard. Step one was to erect our tent. Since it was on the smallish side, it went up easily but it was then that I realized that the tent had been on the wrong side of a "too big" campfire and was filled with burn holes. Not to worry. We had good sleeping bags but upon closer inspection I realized that they were "summer" sleeping bags. They had the insulation of a bed sheet.

It was cold so I wanted to get the fire going. We set off to gather some nice logs but all we could find was fallen trees and they were soaked through with melted snow. Nothing was dry. I chopped up some branches and gathered some paper from the car to light a fire. No luck. We could not get the fire to start. Linda was freezing by now and I knew that my introduction to camping needed to get better in a hurry. I knew that warmth is a requirement for a happy woman so I decided to help the fire along with some white gas from the Coleman stove. I wadded up the last of our newspaper and buried it beneath a pile of the smallest twigs I could find and lit it. I could quickly see that the paper alone was not going to light my wood twigs so I grabbed the can of white gas and poured it on the fire.

This method is not recommended in the Wolf or Bear Cub Scout manuals. Instantly, the flames shot up about four feet. Since Linda was leaning over the fire pit, the flames hit her full in the face and singed her eyebrows and the front of her hair. Not good. The flames were quickly extinguished so there were no burns but she couldn't seem to get over having no eyebrows. Since it was now about 8PM and our dinner consisted of things that had to be heated up and since it would have taken almost two hours to get to the closest restaurant, we decided it was time for bed.

No dinner. Burned eyebrows. Cold. Wet. Forest noises. Summer sleeping bags. Needless to say I was unable to convince her that we should zip our sleeping bags together that night. The following morning we packed up our tent and supplies and lugged everything to the car. I don't remember what we discussed on the way back to Seattle but I am sure that planning our next camping trip was not included.

As of this writing we have been married 42 years and our camping trips together still number just one.

Hawaii

Things were now starting to stabilize in our lives. We had moved (once again) to a house on Queen Anne Hill in Seattle. I had my journeyman's license. Linda had a good job. We were starting to settle down. But, settling down just doesn't seem to fit our lifestyle so we decided to set out on an "around the world" working tour.

We decided our first stop would be Hawaii. Neither of us had ever been there and it certainly looked like paradise in the travel magazines. As a full fledged journeyman electrician I could get work basically anywhere in the world (assuming there was work to be done). In the trades, it is called "booming", which means you just follow the work around the world. We decided that since the economy was going full tilt and we had no kids, it was a great time to "go booming". So, we sold our house in Seattle and bought plane tickets. We had no idea where we would live but we had heard that there was lots of work in Honolulu so off we went. We parked our car in a friend's garage and put what we couldn't carry in storage. We moved to Hawaii with five suitcases. We ended up living for seven months on just the things we brought with us in those five suitcases.

So here we were, standing in the Honolulu airport, not knowing what to do next. We got a cab and asked to be taken to downtown Waikiki. That was our master plan—a cab to Waikiki. He dropped us off at a nice looking hotel right on the water and we checked in. I had no idea how long it would take to get work but I wanted to get my name on the list as soon as possible. That way we could "vacation" until something opened up.

I looked up the address of the electrician's union hall and it was close by so we walked over so I could sign the book. When I got there the union hall was empty. That usually means bad news—there is no work at all—but I walked up to the business manager's desk and said I would like to work. He asked for my journeyman card and checked me in. He then asked when I would like to start (a promising question) and I said "any time." He said, "OK, be at this address at 3PM today." I stammered out that we had only arrived and didn't even have a place to live yet and didn't expect to start work so soon. We hadn't even had lunch! He responded with the comment "I guess they can wait until tomorrow morning at 7AM, *if that works for you.*" I felt like I needed to apologize for not bringing my tools with me but 7AM the following day found me on a jobsite just minutes from where our hotel was.

We stayed at the hotel for several more days while Linda looked for an apartment. She found a place right next door to my jobsite, which meant we could get along without a car. Excellent. Well, not so excellent.

It turned out the place had been condemned and people were living there on kind of an "until the city throws you out" basis. The previous tenant had rebuilt his motorcycle engine in the living room and there was a ten-foot wide circle of degreaser in the room. We scrubbed and scrubbed with industrial strength cleaners but the concrete held on to the oil slick. The place was infested with roaches but that was OK because it was also a breeding ground for geckos and they eat roaches. There were no operable windows because termites had eaten away all the casings. The owners just nailed odd shaped windows to what wood was left. We applied illegal bug killer every Sunday morning. All food was kept in plastic containers in the refrigerator. We didn't realize it but we lived in a slum. It worked for us though because we were in paradise and we were together.

And paradise it was. I did work ten-hour days six days a week but we had every Sunday to explore and we loved it. We bought used bicycles and that extended our travel capability considerably. Every now and then we would rent a car and "drive the loop" around the island. After a couple of months we bid farewell to the condemned units and found a very pretty apartment further out of town. Linda walked to work at Sears in the Ala Moana Shopping Center and I rode my bike to work and back.

We have often commented that our time in Hawaii, away from everyone we knew, allowed us to build our lives together.

We have been a team ever since.

The Walk to U of H

So, here we were in Hawaii working six 10-hour days. That meant a lot of overtime and not much time to spend the money. Even in Hawaii, it is hard to spend a whole paycheck on Sunday so as a result the bank account grew. We knew we would need the money because we had no idea what work would be like after Hawaii. We imagined that China was our next stop although we had done no investigative work to determine where our next stop would be. We were truly on a "where the wind blows us" travel program.

We had been in Hawaii for about six months. It was a workday but I wasn't working. I had just been fired from my job because I refused to work on a 440 volt hot panel. I still marvel that I had the guts to refuse this dangerous assignment but I did refuse. There must have been someone else at the union hall that was willing to risk his life so they fired me. Linda was working so I decided to go for a walk. The University of Hawaii sat on a high hill about two miles away from our apartment. We had seen it many times in the distance but had never gone to explore. I decided to take the hike up the hill to the U of H to see what it was like. It was a long straight sidewalk and there was nobody else out and around; except for one person and he was walking just up ahead of me. I caught up with him and struck up a conversation. It turned out he was a professor at the University and was on his way to his office. As we walked he asked what I was doing in Hawaii and how I happened to get there. He was a good listener. I told him my life story over the next hour as we walked.

We arrived at the UofH and he showed me his office and made some coffee for us. Then he said a very curious thing. He said, "I believe you should go back to school and become an architect." Say What??? He went on to explain that he sensed my real interest was in creating something new, something of my own imagination rather than building things that were designed by someone else. In less than two hours, this professor convinced me that it was my destiny to return to school and get my degree—in architecture.

The walk back home took very little time. My mind was swimming with questions on how I could get readmitted to college. What would Linda think? Could we afford it? How could we leave Hawaii when we were having so much fun? I had never liked studying and had always earned grades below average. Even if I did get admitted somewhere, could I actually do the work? I was now 23 and all the other sophomores would be 18 or 19. Wouldn't they have more stamina and be able to study longer hours? Geeze, this was not an easy thing to get my mind around.

When I got back to the apartment Linda was home. We sat down and talked about my morning walk and discussion. She looked me in the eyes and said that I could do anything I set my mind to and she would support me all the way. What a woman!

We started making plans for getting me back to college.

Back to School

I have to admit that getting off the plane in Seattle did feel refreshing. For once, we weren't sweating. Of course it was September but in Hawaii we had gotten used to three showers a day just to stay cool. The little nip in the air felt good. We collected our car and rented a U-Haul truck and we were off to Yakima.

I didn't pick Yakima Valley Community College (YVJC had been renamed YVCC) as the place to restart my education. It was the *only* place that would take me. When I left Yakima Valley Junior College five years earlier, I never expected to return to college—or Yakima for that matter. So, once I decided to move to Seattle, I just *left*. Since it happened to be in the middle of a school quarter when I left, I ended up with 15 hours of F for that quarter. One would think this could have hurt my GPA a lot but in my case it didn't bring the grade average down much because it was already so low. So, YVCC it was until I could get my average up to at least a 2.0 (a long ways to go it turned out). I worked really hard for the next two quarters at YVCC and got straight A's. This brought my average *just* up to 2.0. By now I had enough credits to graduate from YVCC with an Associate Degree but my grade average wasn't good enough to get me into a four-year school. Bummer.

By now, Linda had a good job with the ASCS (Agriculture Stabilization and Conservation Service), which is a long way of saying "the government will pay you farmers to not grow anything." We were all pretty sure there was too much wheat in the world anyway so it was an important job to do. With Linda in a stable job and me not working the number of available four-year schools began to shrink. Central Washington State College was just 30 miles away in Ellensburg and after several letters begging to be admitted, they accepted me.

The daily commute to Ellensburg was anything but easy. The only way to get there was through something called the Ellensburg Canyon, which was a 35-mile road with more turns than a drunken snake. We always kissed the ground when we finally finished the one-hour drive—happy to have survived another trip through the canyon. I found there were several other high school friends that had traveled the same path as I and were headed back to school at Ellensburg while living in Yakima. Two of these were Reed Johnson and Ross Cadigan.

Reed, Ross and I carpooled for most of two years. We tried to not get late afternoon classes so that we could make it home before the 4-5PM rush in the Canyon. It seemed that at least one of us would get stuck with a late class though so the other two of us would go to the local Pizza Hut to "study" while we waited. We were, of course, now well over 21 so we studied while we drank beer. This meant that one of us (the one with the late class) became the "designated driver" while the other two just didn't care how long it took to drive home. Usually we were sobered up by the time we got home to our hard working wives. I think they really wondered why we didn't get more studying done in the afternoons.

I finally graduated in 1972 with a BA in Economics and a second major in Speech Communications. I loved both those subjects. The odd thing about my second major in Speech Communications is that I never once gave a public speech - not in front of the class or any place else.

It always seemed odd to me that you could almost graduate with a degree in Speech without ever giving one.

Keith and Keith

When we moved back to Yakima so I could attend Yakima Valley Community College, we moved into a "half way underground" apartment on the busy street of 16th Avenue. In fact, the very first night we were there, we learned that we were right where everyone shifted to second gear. And, it was uphill so everyone was giving the engine lots of gas. And, we were close to the college and a high school so there were lots of loud "teenage" cars. Our bedroom was maybe 10 feet from this power shifting, gas pedal stomping busy street. Needless to say, we didn't get much sleep that first night (or any other night).

So, after probably three months of no sleep, I visited the office at the college that kept a list of places for rent. They had just the thing. The gal read the notice to me—Very quiet, spacious, private parking, close to school and *zero* rent. A free place. I couldn't believe my luck. The gal then told me "the rest of the story". The free rent was an apartment over the Keith and Keith Funeral Home and the rent was free because it was our responsibility to *always* be home from 9PM to 7AM. Why, I asked, was it so important to be home during those hours? Well, it turns out there is a Washington State law that says that someone must be in attendance at every funeral home during every hour of the day and night. Why? Because there must be someone to roll out the bodies in case of a fire! I knew this would be kind of a hard sell to Linda but once she saw the nice apartment and once I assured her that I would be in charge of the "rolling out" duties, she agreed. We moved in and enjoyed peace and quiet for the first time in months. And, no rent payments. And, closer to school. It was just perfect (almost).

By the way, there never was a fire and Linda never had to help with a "rollout".

The Rose Place House

After about six months at Keith and Keith, we had caught up on our sleep and we really missed going out at night. We also missed having our own place so we started looking around for a house to buy. We lucked out *big time* (we thought) when one of my classmates offered to sell her house to us. It was a 1,000 square foot A frame and was in a nice neighborhood and she would carry the paper. This meant that we didn't have to try to get qualified by a bank. Since Linda was the only one working and I would be in school for at least another year, this looked like the only way we were going to get a house of our own. We worked out a payment plan with Anne (the owner) and we became the proud owners of our new home. True, we weren't sure where the $212 mortgage payment was going to come from but we were once again in our own place.

The house was simple. It was just a rectangular box (40' X 25') with one main support beam going down the center to hold up the sloping roof. The ends of the house were just nailed on once the A frame was complete.

There were just a few issues with the house. Right away we noticed that it seemed somewhat drafty and upon inspection we found there was no insulation in either the walls or the ceiling. Our first winter month our heating bill was $250! Yipes! We would set the thermostat to 68 and the furnace would just never turn off. We finally determined that we could live in the place at a comfortable 60 degrees. That was the best the furnace could do. The furnace and lack of insulation weren't the only issues though.

On the first day of spring, the clothes dryer caught on fire. Fortunately, it was just sheets and I was able to put the fire out and throw the sheets out on the front lawn where they continued to smolder for several hours. I removed the dryer and took it to the front lawn also to let it air out. Disconnecting the dryer uncovered the strangest connection setup I had ever seen. In addition to the gas pipe to the dryer there was a cold-water hose and a drain. Now, why in the world would a dryer need a water pipe and drain? Turns out, the dryer didn't have a vent but, instead, had a weird box where lint would collect then periodically be flushed down the drain with water. What a crazy system. So, of course the fire started when the solenoid to flush the lint failed to work and the lint caught on fire from the gas flame.

As I was inspecting all this extra plumbing, I noticed that the floor was really "squishy". Sure enough, there apparently had been a leak in the water hose for several years and the floor was totally rotted out. I got out my hammer and saw and soon had the entire floor of the utility room removed. Before putting down the new floor, I had to install a dryer vent and remove the water pipe so I traced the pipe back to the hot water heater. But, wait a minute; there *was* no water heater in the house! How could a house not have a water heater? How could we be getting hot water with no water heater anywhere? Where was the damn thing? Turns out, some previous owner had deemed it a good idea to box in the water heater so it wouldn't detract from the closet it was built into. I had to destroy the closet in one of the bedrooms to get to the water heater.

Once I got it opened up, I found that there must have been a leak in the water heater because someone had replaced the pressure relief valve with a solid steel plug. This meant that without a way of releasing pressure, our water heater was really a potential bomb waiting to explode. I realized that we were now buying a new dryer *and* a new water heater in addition to a new floor in the utility room. At least the heating bills were beginning to drop with the coming of spring so we turned the thermostat down to 56 and bought a new water heater and dryer.

But our experience wasn't the worst. Our neighbor next door woke up one morning that same winter to a really cold house. He walked out into his living room to see *snow* piled up along the end wall inside the house. He looked up to see that the entire A frame end to the house had broken away from the rest of the house and was leaning out at about a five percent tilt. He had a three-foot gap at the peak of his roof! It was about this time that we realized that all the houses in our neighborhood were built to the same quality standard by a "reputable" California contractor. I think his claim to fame was that he could finish a house in less than 30 days. He did our whole neighborhood that way. We realized that it was time to "cut and run" and we put the house on the market just as soon as it got warm enough to show the place.

The house did sell and it was a California couple that bought it. We thought that was somehow appropriate.

The First Job

With my college degree in hand, I was ready for my first job. Wow. Of course my first job had *nothing* to do with Economics or even Speech Communications. It was computer programming for which I had no formal training. The job was at Simcoe Heating and Air Conditioning and the owner (Dwight Specker) had allowed me to work at his place (for free) while I completed a Special Study Course. The special study was to determine how the new Wang programmable calculators could be used in a sheet metal shop. Man, this was about as far from economics or speech as one could get but I was taking an advanced statistics class as a part of my economics studies and the new Wang computers had a lot of statistical formulas built right in. They were very cool and I found I loved to play with them. Dwight bought one of the first ones off the line and as such, we were all in the bleeding edge realm. We talked several times with An Wang, the president and founder of Wang Labs trying to debug problems with his new programmable calculators.

The first major project that Dwight wanted to do as a real employee was a simple payroll program. Dwight wanted us to do the payroll "in house" rather than use some outside service. It was my task to figure out how to use the Wang programmable calculators to do this task. Learning the programming wasn't so hard but the business challenge of payroll was a bugger. I had several visits from the union representatives when my program would calculate pay incorrectly. I learned that if you want to meet a lot of union people in a hurry, just screw up their paychecks.

Once the payroll program was behind us, we tackled other more interesting projects. Dwight had a degree in mechanical engineering and he wrote a program for the Wang computer that would do pipe sizing for controlled atmosphere cold storage buildings. These were used in Yakima to keep apples and other fruit fresh for up to a year. His program was very complex and reduced the engineering time from days to mere minutes. He was a genius.

Dwight died of a stroke at his drafting table in the middle of the night at his home. I will always remember him as being a fair and generous person.

Burroughs

After Dwight passed away, I stayed with Simcoe Heating until a new owner was found and the torch had been passed. Dwight had introduced me to computers and I was hooked. I had to have more contact with "big iron". But what company was best? I had no experience interviewing for a job. Rick Pinnell was a high school friend and his dad, George, owned Pinnell Office Machines. I liked George. He had been nice to me the few times I had been to his store so I went to him to ask for advice. Should I seek out a small company (like Simcoe and Pinnells') or should I look to a large company for my next job.

His advice was immediate—go with a big company that will invest money in your training. Then quit and form your own company. George was truly a man who lived that advice. So, I starting looking and found Burroughs Corporation. Yes, they would send me to school for training. Yes, they manufactured computers so I would get to play with those great new machines. And, yes, they had an opening in Yakima!

I started in 1974 with Burroughs as a Sales Trainee. That is what it said on my business card—Alan Churchill—Trainee. Wow, did that instill confidence in whomever I was talking with? Hmmm. Not sure.

My first week was spent studying the "corporate procedural manual" which was 500 pages of shear drivel and totally unused by anyone after their first week of work. When I finally talked to the boss about why I was wasting my time reading this book, he responded that the Regional Sales Manager who would be my immediate boss was off at a sales meeting and would be back the following Monday. Sure enough, the Big Man (Rick Sherman) came through the door Monday morning and I was ready to start making sales calls talking to fortune 500 companies about million dollar machines.

"Not so fast, sonny," he said. First, let's get you some pavement experience. I couldn't understand what selling computers had to do with street repair but I was eager to find out.

And I did. Pavement Experience is a Burroughs term for "give the new guy a ten key calculator to sell and let's see if he ever comes back to the office." Not only that but my territory was Ellensburg so not only did I not get to sell computers but also I had to drive to Ellensburg every day. Just to put things into perspective, I was selling a ten key calculator in a cheap plastic case for $250. This was when anyone could go to the local stationery store and get something better for $99.95. I was shell-shocked. I was selling these things "door to door". Fortunately we focused on business accounts but it was gruesome. I would walk in the door of a business and hand them my "trainee" business card and ask if the manager or owner was in. The person at the front desk would look at the calculator under my arm and try to break it to me gently. "We're not in the market for any calculators right now. Thanks anyway." It was hopeless. Each day I would drive back to Yakima with the same calculator I had left with. My manager, Rick, would point out that I simply had to "tune up" my sales presentations so that the people would *want* what I had to sell. These little pep talks usually lasted no more than 15 minutes and I was sent off with a "Winners never Quit and Quitters never Win" slogan to carry me through the day.

Well, along about my third week, I was getting gas and noticed that the calculator on the station desk was an old 100 key monster. I assumed it didn't work and sure enough, when I asked the station owner if he wouldn't like to have a nice new Burroughs calculator rather than that old piece of junk, he said he *would*. He asked "how much" and I squeaked out $250. Then he asked how much I would give him as a trade-in and quickly added that he wouldn't take a dime less than $100. I applied all my sales skills I had learned and then a miracle happened. He said he would take it. He slapped $150 in cash in my hand and together we lugged the old monster to the trunk of my car. I had no idea if Burroughs would ever approve a trade-in but I determined I would buy it myself if that is what it took. I was so excited I headed back to the office to give them all the good news. I had finally sold something!

It was only 2PM when I burst through the door of the office. "*I sold a calculator*" were my first words. I fully expected a small band to break out in celebration and hear an announcement about my pending promotion to manager of the world. But all I heard from Rick was "What the *hell* are you doing back in the office at 2PM? This is *prime selling time*." And out the door I went. Of course it was too late to drive back to Ellensburg so I went home and told Linda. She was overjoyed. After a little celebration with her, I went back to the office (at 4:45PM) and again announced that I had sold a calculator. This time Rick's response was very congratulatory. He wanted to know all the details and when I got to the part about the trade-in he laughed and asked me where I thought all those junk calculators came from that we had in the back storage room. "Heck," he said, "We feel lucky to get more than $100 on any calculator sale after discounts. You did good getting $150." The world seemed all right after that.

Once I had hit quota on calculator sales (it took 6 months) I was qualified for my first real training session. Burroughs had basically taken over a Holiday Inn in Pasadena, CA and did all their training there. They sent me down for two full weeks of training. Four salesmen shared one room. There were people from all over the country. We learned every sales skill known to man in just two weeks and came home ready to tackle the world. By now I had moved up to "electro-mechanical accounting machines" which were the size of a desk, cost $25,000 and made as much noise as a small railroad engine. It took only two sales a year to make quota so that tells you pretty quickly how much money the salesman made. Not much.

But, along with the sale of the machine came the sale of lots of consumables. Paper punch tape (just like Dad used to bring home), ledger cards with a magnetic ink strip down the side, checks etc. I was wondering how much commission we got on those "never ending" revenue streams when I was informed that the Burroughs Company had a special division to handle those things. I did get a commission but only on the machine itself. Everything else after the initial sale went to someone else. Bummer. I was beginning to question George Pinnell's advice about big companies.

But then something happened. Burroughs came out with a mini computer. It was a miracle of progressiveness complete with flashing lights and 8" diameter floppy disks. It was being sold for the *same price* as our electro-mechanical monsters and could do four times the work. There wasn't a company in the world that could live without this Burroughs B-80 computer. So, off to Pasadena I went for two more weeks of training. This time it was all about the B-80. Our enthusiasm waned a little when we found out that the training center had one repairman per machine just to keep the machines working. Apparently, there were a few little glitches left in the new computer. We finished our training and headed back to the real world where we found that not *every* company in America had to have one of our new B-80 machines. But, enough companies did decide that it was a better deal than the old noisy electro-mechanical monsters we had sold them only months before.

The computer age was upon us and I was right in the middle of it.

Flint's Arrival

By 1972, Linda and I had been married four years and we were starting to think about a family. We had always been interested in the Asian culture and so started looking into adoption of an Asian child. We found the Holt organization and really liked the fact that they had such a strong focus on helping children. We applied and were put on a waiting list of one year. We later found out that all adoption applicants are put into a one-year holding pattern just to make sure the prospective parents are really serious. So, after our one-year wait, we met with a counselor who looked us over pretty good. Then we got on another waiting list, which lasted another year. Finally we got word that we had been accepted and a baby had been selected for us. It was a boy (fairly uncommon) and his name was Boo Hyun Chul. We named him Flint because we thought that it would be difficult for school kids to make up a funny rhyming name for Flint.

At that time, the Holt program delivered the babies to an airport in the US convenient for the new parents. For us, Seattle was the closest one so August 9, 1974, we drove to Seattle with our little car loaded up with blankets, warm milk (which ended up soured), books on how to "parent" and diapers. We had rented a videotape camera to use at the airport but failed to check the batteries. Turned out the batteries lasted right up until Flint was brought off the plane and that was the end of our videotaping. We did get some movie footage of planes landing and taking off before Flint arrived. Small consolation.

And here he came in the arms of a very tired volunteer. We sat in the airport for about an hour playing with our new six-month-old baby and getting to know the other new parents. There were about eight babies delivered that day to Seattle.

At the time, Linda's sister lived in Bellevue so we drove over there to show off Flint to the whole family. Everyone wanted a chance to hold Flint and exclaim how beautiful he was. Of course, Seoul is 12 hours behind us so for Flint, it was the middle of the night and he wanted to sleep. No chance. Too many excited family members to let that happen.

Finally, at around 5PM we decided to hit the road for the three-hour drive to Yakima. Flint slept the whole way although his stomach was severely challenged by the sour milk we gave him.

Finally, we arrived home in a state of near exhaustion ready for sleep. However, Flint was now awake and ready for a "new day". His day had finally started! That first night there was no sleep for anyone in our household. The next night, same thing. Then finally, on the third day, complete exhaustion hit all of us at once and we all finally got some sleep. Our dog, Angus, even liked the new addition to the family.

Over the following few weeks, Flint became familiar to our time zone, our food, our milk and everything else American. We had well-meaning friends ask if he spoke any Korean to which we responded that both his English and Korean were about even at this time in his life.

Flint Chuchill in 1980.

The adoption counselor continued her visits (a nerve wracking time) and at one of those meetings she suggested it would be fun to have some other adoptive families over for a party. It sounded good to us so we told her to go ahead and invite all the adoptive families she knew. We would be happy to host it. Little did we know she knew a *lot* of adoptive families. We eventually had 60 people in our house. It was about 20 families and they had kids from everywhere around the world. It was a very interesting time. Linda made lasagna (four huge pans of it) and everyone ate off paper plates on the floor or standing up. Through all that commotion, there wasn't one thing spilled on the carpets or furniture. It was amazing. A good time was had by all.

The Bouncing Baby

From the day Flint arrived, he was athletic. As with most six month olds, he had already learned to crawl and he kept both of us running to keep up with him. We had moved to a big three story English Tudor house on Yakima Avenue and all the bedrooms were upstairs. It was an older house with hardwood floors in all the upstairs rooms.

Flint's first bed, of course, was a crib. We put the sides up nice and high so he couldn't get out and felt secure that he was safe. Oh, what parents don't know. Linda and I would put him down at night and read him a story and then sneak out of the room and head downstairs.

A nice thing about hardwood floors is that you can hear when things are dropped or thrown out of a crib and Flint loved to gather up all his toys that he had in his crib and throw them out. So, downstairs, we would hear one thing after another hit the floor. Then along about age two, Flint realized that he could jump up and down in his crib if he wasn't ready to go to sleep. He would hold onto the side of the crib and bounce and bounce and bounce like on a trampoline. We could hear the springs in the crib being tested as each bounce went higher and higher.

And then one night, our little athlete *really* did not want to go to sleep. He held onto the side of the crib and bounced with all his might until, oh-oh, he bounced right out of the crib and came crashing down on the hardwood floor. It sounded to us like the roof had fallen in. Linda and I ran up the stairs to rescue him but when we opened his door, there he was in the middle of he floor with a big smile on his face. Apparently the pain he must have suffered when falling three feet from his crib was outweighed by the new knowledge that he could escape from his crib.

The next day we went shopping for a "big boy" bed with no side rails. We struck a deal whereby he would never jump on his big boy bed. Flint had grown up just a little.

Katie's Arrival

By the time Flint was two, we were starting to think about a second child. Flint had turned out to be such a good experience that we went back to Holt for "round two". We were informed that even though we were now experienced parents, the one year wait was still in effect. So we waited another year before our application was processed. And, of course, the approval process still took another year. So, by the time we finally got Katie (Eun Yee Cho), two full years had passed.

This time, though, the Korean government had figured out that US adoptive parents had money to spend and it seemed reasonable to them that they should come to Korea to spend some of it. So, we decided that Linda would make the trip to Seoul and I would stay home with Flint. While she was in Korea, she was introduced to the culture of the country, the food, the Bridge of No Return that went between North and South Korea, a tour of the Holt Adoptive Agency and the four gates, which had been turned into giant markets. Every day Linda was busy with "touring" but got only one visit with our new daughter, Katie.

Then, on the last day, the whole group of about 10 adoptive parents made an early morning trip to Holt. They picked up their new babies then were hurried in the back door of the airport with their children. Some Korean people did not approve of allowing their children to be adopted by "foreigners" and the adoption people didn't want any disruption at that late date. The trip lasted two weeks and it was to be my first experience of being a single father. It wasn't easy but things must have gone OK because both Flint and I made it through the test.

On June 13, 1978, Linda and Katie arrived home to Yakima after more than 36 hours of travel and no sleep. She was exhausted. At that time, the airport in Yakima still had the steps that wheeled out to the plane and the travelers had to walk across the tarmac to the terminal. I waited and waited and waited for the door of the plane to open. The stewardesses must have arranged for Linda to get off first because there she was with a little crying bundle in her arms. She staggered down the stairs in slow motion and looked like she was in a daze as she made her way across the pavement to the doors of the terminal. Finally she saw me and broke into tears. She got to the double doors to the terminal building and that is all the energy she had. She collapsed with Katie in her arms right in the middle of the doorway. With all her bags and blankets and Katie, she took up the whole doorway. Nobody could pass. I rushed to pick her up and found she was like a damp rag. Linda was totally spent. Katie was crying. Flint started crying and it was total confusion. We finally moved (dragged) Linda and Katie and all her bags off to a corner and got reassembled. Flint, now a big brother, picked up the bags. I picked up Linda in one arm and Katie in the other and we headed home.

Linda slept for two full days. Katie finally stopped crying and Flint seemed to

Katie Churchill in 1978 one year after she arrived.

grow up overnight. Over the next few weeks, Linda finally told me all of her experiences in Seoul but of course the best experience was picking up Katie on that last day.

That was over 34 years ago but I still remember that day clearly.

Katie, Jon and Scissors

We moved to Tigard, OR in 1980 to the most wonderful neighborhood we had ever seen. It was brand new and many of the residents on our cul-de-sac were our age with young children. We quickly met and liked everyone. Kids, of course, bring families together and soon we were best friends with the Worsley family who lived just three doors away. Their kids were the same age as our kids. Our Katie (then three) just loved Jon Worsley who was also three. They played with each other constantly. Since Dona (the Mom) and Linda stayed at home with the kids, Katie and Jon were constant companions.

Dona and Linda also became good friends but there was one incident that enhanced (tested) that friendship. It was a nice summer day and the kids were playing at the Worsley home. Dona was sewing and realized that the kids had become really quiet. That is always a dangerous sign. Screams of fear and pain pale in comparison to the sound of quiet children. And there was *no* noise coming out of the bedroom where Katie and Jon had gone to play.

Dona wisely decided it was time for a little investigation.

Linda was home that day and was surprised to look up and see Katie standing in the doorway looking very sad and maybe guilty. Linda could tell something was wrong. With a little questioning, Katie admitted that Dona had told Katie it was time to go home. Something just didn't sound right to Linda so he headed over to Dona's house to investigate further.

When Dona answered the door, she didn't look any too happy either. It turned out that Jon and Katie had decided to cut out the characters on Jon's new Sesame Street bed sheets. Dona still marvels at how much cutting Katie and Jon (mostly Katie) could do in so few minutes. Dona assured Linda that she could sew everything back together.

The one good thing that came of the scissors and bed sheet experience was that Flint *loved* it and thought Katie was a genius for thinking that up.

The Worsleys are still living in the same house and we are still best friends with them. Jon and Katie still see each other on occasion but Dona puts away the scissors when Katie comes to visit. I guess she figures better safe than sorry (again).

Timberline

As a Burroughs salesman I got introduced to many software companies. This was because Burroughs pretty much just sold the hardware and left software to other companies. Burroughs executives had determined that there was no money in software and that hardware was where the big bucks were. This meant that we were always working with software partners to sell our machines.

One such company was Timberline Systems. It was headquartered in Beaverton, OR. I made many joint sales calls with the Timberline sales people because they had a great client write-up package for accountants and a very popular construction job cost package for construction companies. Timberline was founded by a couple of really great guys—John Gorman and Hap Clarke. John was the business side and Hap was the technical side. Together they made a wonderful team.

In my second year as a Burroughs salesman, I sold more Burroughs computers with Timberline software than I did with any other software company. Timberline was recognized as the dream company to work for in the software field. They had a knockdown sales manager named Dick Wissmiller who hired some of the best salesmen known to software. The group eventually included Jim Allen, Larry Briggs, Sam Coluccio, Neil Anderson, John Naab, Dennis Koster, Jim Campbell, Steve Woslewski, Nace Mullen, Ted Feierstein, Dale Thomas, Mike Steding, Ollie Renner, Bill LeSeur and (later) Mike Ayersman, Terry Hutt and me. These people could outsell any other sales force on the planet. As an example, Jim Allen sold $1,200,000 in software in 1977 when the average sale was $15,000. It earned him a new BMW paid for by Timberline. It was unbelievable.

It was inevitable that I would want to go to work for John and his company of super stars. Everybody wanted to work there. So, I took my Burroughs sales reports for the past two years with me for a visit to the hallowed ground of software—Beaverton. I could scarcely believe my ears when John said he would *love* to have me come to work at Timberline. And, he said I could stay right in Yakima and take the territory of Eastern WA and Alberta. I didn't know if there was much going on in Alberta and the only town of any size in eastern Washington was Spokane but I was so excited about the opportunity that I said yes and joined the company. It turned out to be the single most important move I would ever make in my professional career.

I loved the company and its people. I loved the software. I even loved the customer base, which was accountants and contractors. It was no wonder I did well. I loved every second of my workday and the sales figures climbed and climbed. I found that we had a *very* good Burroughs salesman in Lethbridge, Alberta - a small town about two hours south of Calgary. Iain Smith was the only Burroughs salesman in Lethbridge and he soon began to take up more of my time. It seemed like every trip North to Lethbridge resulted in a sale. Linda and I soon decided to move to Spokane to make the commute to Canada easier. I ended up getting on a plane every Tuesday morning and coming back on Thursday afternoon—and always with one or two more orders for software. It was just fantastic. It wasn't long before people at Timberline started to notice. What were Iain Smith and Alan Churchill doing up in Canada that made such an impact? Truth was that Iain was doing it all but John Gorman got it into his head that he needed me down in Beaverton as his National Sales Manager. John had the mistaken belief that a good salesman would automatically be a good sales manager.

And so it was in 1980 that I made the move to Oregon. Linda stayed behind in Spokane to sell the house and get the kids through the end of school. I ended up living in the Greenwood Gardens hotel for six months while I worked 16-hour days at the office and Linda managed the house in Spokane.

We finally sold the house and Linda came to Beaverton to start the search for a new home. On the third day, she found a beauty. It cost *twice* what we got for our home in Spokane but it was brand new and it was empty and we were rich. We slapped down the down payment and we were Oregonians for the first time.

We had no idea what highs and lows were just ahead of us.

Mike Ayersman

One of my first moves as the new sales manager was to go looking for new sales talent. The first person I thought of was Mike Ayersman who had become a good friend while I was at Burroughs. Mike worked in the Richland/Pasco/Kennewick area of eastern Washington. He was stuck in a little dinky office with no real chance for expansion unless he moved to some other city. Since I had left Spokane, we were looking for the right person for that office and Mike was my pick. I worked and worked and worked on Mike but he wouldn't quit Burroughs. I offered him more money, offered to pay for the move, offered him a bigger and better territory. Nothing worked until I realized that he was in love with Eileen and would probably do whatever she thought would be best. I started to work on Eileen and finally my efforts paid off. We got Mike to take the Spokane territory in 1980.

In April of 1982 we had a sales management opening in the Dallas/Ft.

Mike Ayersman and Alan met again for the first time in ten years in 2010.

Worth office and once again, my first choice was Mike. I called him and asked if he wouldn't like to come to Beaverton for a few days of "management meetings." Mike agreed and I met him at the Portland airport. Those were the days when you could go all the way to the loading area without a ticket so I met Mike at the gate. Rather than exiting to the parking area, we walked over to another gate that was going to Dallas. Mike asked if we were meeting someone else at the airport and I said we were taking a "little detour" on our way to Beaverton. The "little detour" was a trip to Dallas where I would have two full days to convince Mike that he and Eileen needed to move to Texas! Off we went and we spent the time visiting Dallas, Austin and meeting with the sales people that Mike would manage. Although it took two months to convince Mike (and Eileen) that Texas was just *wonderful*, they finally saw the light and Mike said yes. As expected, Mike did an outstanding job and brought many new customers to the Timberline fold. He stayed in Dallas for three years, which went past my time at Timberline.

As had happened before in my life, the people I associated with had a big impact on me. With Mike, it was definitely a positive impact.

What Price Success?

But not all was peaches and cream at work back in Beaverton. True, our sales were still rising but competitors had found our little niche and were making us work harder for each sale. The company went through two "black Friday" meetings where we would pass around the employee list with the instructions from John that we had to eliminate 10% of the company roster. These were the most depressing meetings I had ever attended. Timberline was like a family. We knew everyone personally but times were tough and the money wasn't flowing in the door as it had in past years. Jim Allen, Dale Thomas and Dick Wissmiler had moved on to other endeavors. The magic was gone. The sales force that Jim had hired did not respond to my management skills like they did to his. In fact, he had sales management skills and mine were lacking. My workweek increasingly took me on the road. Over the next two years I visited nearly every state in the Union interviewing and hiring new sales candidates.

    I experienced the feeling that most every professional traveler experiences—that of waking up and not knowing what city I was in. When I would come into town, we would usually have a sales dinner, which always involved a lot of drinking. And, these sales trips were never ending. I was out with the boys nearly every night in towns hundreds or thousands of miles away from my family. When I would get home I was exhausted and spent much of my time sleeping. It was a grueling lifestyle and I finally could do it no longer. I was on the road so much that my travel expenses actually exceeded my income and my income was considerable.

But it wasn't worth it. I just couldn't do "the grind" any more and I resigned. It was a sad ending to a promising career but it was time for a new start - one that would be spent at home every night rather than at some motel.

Unfortunately, the "new start" took over five years to get going. We found that the expensive house that my Timberline income supported quite easily was a burden we could no longer afford. Between the high principal payments and the 14% interest rate, we were in over our head. The house went back to the bank and we moved into a rental for the next two years. I joined a company headed up by Dan Cotton selling Timberline software to Burroughs dealers. Dan had been an executive at Burroughs with a good record but I found him impossible to work for and I left after just a few months. It was a dark time. The family could tell that I had lost my "edge". I couldn't find an employer who could put up with my ego. I was changing jobs constantly. I had gone from being someone important in the business world to someone who was trying to get back on track. The "dark time" finally ended when I realized that the world didn't revolve around me.

The New Start finally kicked into high gear when I found Steve Littlefield and Dimensions Software.

Dimensions

It was now 1986. I had spent four years working almost as a "temporary employee" based on the shortness of many of my jobs. One of those years I had four employers listed on my tax return. But in 1986 I found Steve Littlefield and Dimensions Software. They were headquartered in Salt Lake City and had just introduced a software package for hardware stores and lumberyards. It ran on the brand new IBM PC that (as everyone knew) could run only one program at a time. Well, Steve and his people had uncovered a tiny little company called Bluebird Systems that enabled the lowly PC to run up to four terminals at the same time. This meant we could sell a system to a small lumberyard for about 40% less than what a similar mini-computer would sell for. I went to work for Steve and Dimensions as a salesman. My territory was Oregon and Washington. It was like the early days of Timberline all over again. We had a great product and the sales dollars just flowed in the door. Nearly every one of my customers was buying their very first computer.

The Dimensions product was really quite startling in its capability. Steve had a small group of genius programmers that somehow could write code that did exactly what a typical lumberyard owner needed. For the first year (before the rest of the world caught on) we sold an average of two systems per month per salesman. It was phenomenal. We soon found that we had to restrict sales because we had no trainers available. We told customers that they would have to "wait their turn" for the implementation process.

The IBM PC continued to expand with more memory and more disk space and the Bluebird people continued to expand their operating system software to keep pace. The lowly PC coupled with the Bluebird operating system eventually grew to handle a maximum number of 255 users. After Bluebird discontinued their PC offering, Dimensions reworked their software to run on the Unix operating system, which eventually got them to 400 users. Amazing.

As with Timberline, I soon grew tired of traveling so much so I switched jobs to being a trainer for the last three years at Dimensions. I still had to travel but at least I was in one place for several days at a time.

Steve finally sold Dimensions to a software conglomerate but the product is still in use today 25 years after it was first released. The fact that a software product originally written to handle four users could be expanded to 400 users is a strong testament to the far sightedness of Steve and his crew.

Steve Littlefield at his desk in 2009. Still at work doing great software.

Moving

Linda and I were married in November of 1968 and right away we found that we didn't mind moving around from place to place. In fact, in our married life (the first 42 years as of this writing) we have moved 21 times. Those moves took us to eight apartments and 13 homes. We just don't mind moving. To the best of our recollection, here are the places we have lived.

Who	From	To	Address	City	State
Linda	1947	1952	Farm to Market Rd.	Edison	WA
Linda	1952	1965	Rt. 1	Bow	WA
Linda	1965	1966	Dorm at Western	Bellingham	WA
Linda	1966	1966	Summit Ave	Seattle	WA
Linda	1966	1967	On Lake Washington	Seattle	WA
Linda	1967	1967	Belmont St.	Seattle	WA
Linda	1968	1968	North Garden St.	Bellingham	WA
Alan	1946	1951	West Grandview Ave.	Sunnyside	WA
Alan	1951	1965	N 24th Ave.	Yakima	WA
Alan	1965	1965	Denny Way	Seattle	WA
Alan	1965	1966	Summit Ave.	Seattle	WA
Alan	1966	1967	Summit Ave	Seattle	WA
Alan	1967	1967	51st (U District)	Seattle	WA
Together	1968	1968	Green Lake	Seattle	WA
Together	1969	1969	First Ave West	Seattle	WA
Together	1970	1970	Kapiolani Blvd	Honolulu	HI

Together	1970	1970	Ernst St	Honolulu	HI
Together	1971	1971	N 16th Ave.	Yakima	WA
Together	1971	1971	West Yakima Ave.	Yakima	WA
Together	1972	1973	Rose Place	Yakima	WA
Together	1973	1973	W Lincoln	Yakima	WA
Together	1973	1978	West Yakima Ave	Yakima	WA
Together	1978	1979	Bristol Court	Yakima	WA
Together	1979	1980	Clinton Way	Yakima	WA
Together	1980	1981	West Bellwood Drive	Spokane	WA
Together	1981	1983	SW Sylvan Ct.	Tigard	OR
Together	1983	1985	SW Steven Ct.	Tigard	OR
Together	1986	1992	SW 98th Ct.	Tigard	OR
Together	1992	1999	Woodhue St.	Tigard	OR
Together	1999	1999	SW Barrows Rd #1	Tigard	OR
Together	1999	2005	SW Taposa Place	Tualatin	OR
Together	2005	2006	SW 136th Ave.	King City	OR
Together	2006	2006	Stonesthrow Apts	Tualatin	OR
Together	2006	???	SW Cowlitz Dr.	Tualatin	OR

We have talked a lot about the benefits of moving so much. For most of those years we simply "rode the market up" and ended up paying nothing for housing. The increased value exceeded the cost of mortgage payments.

But more importantly, we became attached to each other, not to our houses. We found that moving around a lot kept life interesting.

Writing Your Own Book

My whole family is full of published authors. My grandfather was an author with five books and numerous short stories to his credit. My father was a writer most of his adult life working for the local paper. He started writing books for fun and has three books and several *Readers Digest* articles to his credit. My Mother wrote a very helpful book after my father passed away on how to survive the death of a husband. My sister wrote a book combining recipes and remembrances of being a Bed and Breakfast owner/manager. With all those people in my family writing and publishing and working their fingers to the bone putting out books, you would think that ONE of them would have written down something about how to publish a book. Well, they didn't so here it is.

If you want to write a book, you will need to do the following:

1. Get state and city business licenses, a PO Box, a checking account, debit card and PayPal account that will be dedicated to the book. You will need a web address and hosting agreement. I use GoDaddy.com for these. Have a web page created. I used Betty Weinberg at Zapponet.com for my page. All of this will take about a day and cost around $700.

2. Email Gorham Printing at info@gorhamprinting.com and get your free copy of "A Guide to Book Printing and Self-Publishing. It is a goldmine of info regardless of who you use for printing your book.

3. Get a Library of Congress PCN number and get an ISBN number. Go to Kinkos and scan all your old photos on their Sony self-service machine. All this will take about a day and will cost another $200.

4. Write the book. Set aside about 1-2 hours a day for writing. This book took me six months to complete the rough draft and another month for revisions.

5. Find a set of friends that will serve as your proofreaders. I had six friends do this and each of them found different things to change or fix. Give them a free book for their 10-20 hours of work. You can't afford to pay someone for this work.

6. Find a good book printer and let them do the layout of the whole book including the cover. I used Gorham Printing (www.gorham-printing.com). Figure on $1,000 for the setup services.

7. Use your book printer to print however many copies of your book you think will sell in about three months. I printed 200 books for a little over $900. A printer will require about a month between when you hand him your manuscript and when the book is finished.

8. Price the book for $19.95 retail. If you sell half of them at full retail and the remainder at varying discounts for libraries, bookstores and companies like Amazon, you will end up with revenue and expense being about equal.

So, for basically no long term cost (revenue and expense will be about equal) you will be doing something really enjoyable, you will get out of cleaning the garage for at least six months and you will add one more item to your list of lifetime accomplishments. It sure beats watching daytime TV!

Permissions

I came across the sign below when touring the third grade classroom of Jerroll Shires. The photo is a little grainy but the words are, in my opinion, words to live by whether we are in the third grade or an adult in our golden years. I believe that I have a very enjoyable life and it is due, in part, to adhering to these rules—even though I did not see them written down until just a year ago.

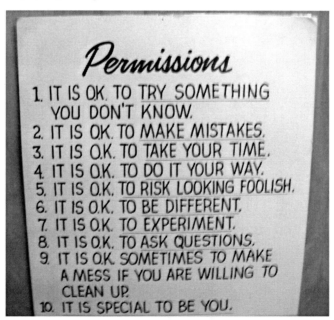

These permissions were posted in the third grade class of Jerroll Shires. I believe they are words to live by.

Lessons Learned

Each of the chapters in this book has a "lesson learned".

I know I can: When attempting a new task, it always pays to seek the guidance of someone older and possibly wiser. If you are going for a record, get a witness.

The Ultimate "Growing Up" House: There are hidden benefits everywhere. Enjoying life as it is happening is the key to happiness.

The Fort: Don't put all your eggs in one basket. Just because you appear to have won a battle doesn't mean you have won the war.

The Challenge of the 7th Grade: Believe in yourself even if nobody else does.

The Challenge of the 8th Grade: Have a broader view of what is really happening in the world. Things are not always as they seem.

Passing my Ham Radio Exam: Dreams can become realities with enough study.

The Science Fair: Sometimes a miracle will happen.

The Desk: How can grandparents sometimes know what the perfect gift is?

Antennas: Stupidity is not always rewarded with death. Sometimes you get lucky and don't fall out of the tree.

Summer Work: A few dollars every day add up. Older people sometimes have interesting and important things to say.

My First Car Phone: Sometimes having the coolest toy really is cool.

Grandview Avenue Grocery: The customer is always right. Trust but verify.

The Party at Robin Paisley's House: If it "feels wrong" it probably is. Don't accept every invitation to every party.

San Francisco with Jerry Stein: Don't ever let your teenage son out of your sight.

Mexico and the Milk Truck: Don't ever let four teenage sons out of your sight.

Breaking In to the State Police: Adults sometimes have a different perspective than kids.

New York World's Fair: Even sophisticated people can be ignorant of current events. Money doesn't buy "worldliness".

Rick Lloyd: A free spirit is a treat for everyone.

Freshman Class President: Slogans get people elected.

School Spirit and the Cannon: Gunpowder and darkness are not a good mix. Police are usually hiding in places you don't expect.

The Move to Seattle: Don't burn bridges when leaving school or employment. You may want to go back there some day.

Dirty, Hungry and Tired: All things in moderation.

Boy Meets Girl: Life is full of surprises. Drink less beer before introducing yourself to people.

The Fire: Gasoline and stupidity are not a good combination. If you like to play with fire, at least live close to a fire station.

Sliding Doors and Flying Saucers: Sometimes you just take your lumps.

The Journeyman Test: Preparation trumps all.

Becoming a Land Baron: Understand your market when setting prices.

The Proposal: Know the answer before asking important questions.

Campout on Saddle Mountain: Prepare or fail. Gas is not a good fire starter.

Hawaii: It really is paradise and can make you blind to the conditions in which you are living.

The Walk to U of H: You just never know what is around the corner or up the hill.

Back to School: Anything is possible with a will to succeed.

Keith and Keith: Don't say *no* too quickly.

The Rose Place House: Don't say *yes* too quickly.

The First Job: Remember that a job is temporary and a family is permanent.

Burroughs: Never give up. Someone somewhere needs a calculator.

Flint's Arrival: Good things come in small packages.

The Bouncing Baby: Laws of physics don't always work in your favor.

Katie's Arrival: Stay with a winning system.

Katie, Jon and Scissors: Beware of quiet children.

Timberline: Don't let your ego take over.

Mike Ayersman: Run with a winner when you find one.

What Price Success? Remember what is really important in life.

Dimensions: Quality people are the most important thing.

Moving: Don't be afraid to take a chance.

Writing your own book: The hardest part is getting started.

Permissions: Life is to be lived each day. Tomorrow will come soon enough.

One last lesson: You may have noticed that this book ends in 1990—about 20 years ago. Does this mean that absolutely nothing happened in my life for the last 20 years? Absolutely not! However, to find out the fascinating details about those 20 years, you will have to wait until Echoes II comes out. But don't wait to buy that book. Order THIS ONE. It may be just the thing that eliminates the need for me to write a chapter about what it is like to be a Walmart greeter!

Jon Worsley and Katie many years after the scissors event.

Flint and Katie circa 1978.

The author with his Mother, Dorothy Churchill in 1964 in front of the 24th Avenue house.

The author with sister Susan and brother Sam in 1951.

The Arecibo Observatory radio telescope located in Puerto Rico. This antenna was used to bounce signals off the moon by ham radio operators. An article on this antenna gave the author the idea for the title to this book.

Dorothy Churchill in April 2008 at 90 years old.

Linda and Alan walk down the aisle in 1968.

The Churchill family just moved into the 24th Avenue house in Yakima circa 1952. Dorothy, Sam Jr., Susan, Sam Sr., Alan.

Hallstatt, Austria. The author's favorite town in the world.

About the Author

Alan Churchill was born in 1946 and was raised in Eastern Washington. This is his fifth book but the first four books never made it out of his head and onto paper, so this is the first one you can actually buy. Alan aspired to a degree in electrical engineering from MIT but his poor marks in grade school pretty much scotched those plans. His experiences were gained from a succession of odd jobs and an association with many different and interesting people. He and his wife Linda have lived in more than 20 different locations over the years and have traveled to a variety of foreign countries. His favorite city is Hallstatt, Austria because of its timeless beauty and peaceful setting.

Alan and Linda currently live in Tualatin, OR where he is retired (retired is the new fired). They have two wonderful children who live close by (but not too close by). Alan decided to start writing when Linda started to make long "honey do" lists to fill his retirement hours. Writing seemed to be an excellent excuse to sit in the easy chair rather than cleaning the garage.

To Order Additional Copies

Additional copies of this book as well as other books published by the Author's family members may be ordered via mail or electronically.

To order via the US Postal Service, make a copy of this page (don't you DARE tear this page out) and mail it along with a check or money order to:

Alan C. Churchill Publishing LLC
PO Box 4201
Tualatin, OR 97062-9997

To order electronically, go to www.alanchurchill.com. Enter the quantity of books desired and then click on the PayPal Buy Now button. You may use a MasterCard, Visa, American Express, Discover or PayPal card. Your payment is via a secure server.

Your order will be shipped within two days of receipt of order.

Email alan@alanchurchill.com with reader comments or questions.

Here are the books (with revisions) written by Roscoe Sheller, Sam Churchill, Dorothy Churchill and Susan Drummond.

ORDER FORM FOR BOOKS FROM THE CHURCHILL FAMILY

Title	Author	Quantity	Price	Extension
Echoes	Alan Churchill		19.95	
Me and the Model T	Roscoe Sheller		19.95	
Ben Snipes NW Cattle King	Roscoe Sheller		19.95	
Blowsand	Roscoe Sheller		19.95	
Don't Call Me Ma	Sam Churchill		19.95	
From Bandit to Lawman	Sam Churchill		19.95	
From Mourning to Morning	Dorothy Churchill		7.95	
The Inn-Siders Cookbook	Susan Drummond		14.95	
Barkley and Betsy	Susan Drummond		14.95	
Shipping and handling—Note just one amount for any quantity of books				5.05
			Total	